HOW TO WIN A MARGINAL SEAT

HOW TO WIN A MARGINAL SEAT

MY YEAR FIGHTING FOR MY POLITICAL LIFE

Gavin Barwell

First published in Great Britain in 2016 by
Biteback Publishing Ltd
Westminster Tower
3 Albert Embankment
London SE1 7SP

ISBN 978-1-78590-047-1

10 9 8 7 6 5 4 3 2 1

A CIP catalogue record for this book is available from the British Library.

Set in Quadraat by Adrian McLaughlin

Printed and bound in Great Britain by
CPI Group (UK) Ltd, Croydon CR0 4YY

To Karen, Jack, Sam & Jamie for putting up with me.

And to everyone who worked on #BackBarwell2015 –
you made the difference.

The credit belongs to the man who is actually in the arena, whose face is marred by dust and sweat and blood; who strives valiantly; who errs, who comes short again and again, because there is no effort without error and shortcoming; but who does actually strive to do the deeds; who knows great enthusiasms, the great devotions; who spends himself in a worthy cause; who at the best knows in the end the triumph of high achievement, and who at the worst, if he fails, at least fails while daring greatly, so that his place shall never be with those cold and timid souls who neither know victory nor defeat.

Contents

Foreword

I'VE NEVER BEEN tempted to write a book before, but in the weeks after the general election on 7 May 2015 the idea slowly began to grow on me.

The contest in my constituency of Croydon Central had been by any measure – the amount of money spent, the frequency of visits by ministers and shadow ministers, the volume of literature delivered or the number of political activists pounding the streets – one of the most intensive constituency campaigns this country has ever seen. At the end of it, I had hung on by the skin of my teeth. The experience had been a gruelling one, both physically and psychologically, from which I was struggling to recover. Here was a story worth telling.

So who is this book for? First and foremost, it's for my kids. When they're a bit older, I'd like them to understand what their dad was up to when he wasn't around – and why he was often grumpy when he was. Three young boys is a fairly niche market for a book, however.

It's also for the people who worked on my campaign. I got to stand on the stage and be declared the winner, but I couldn't have done it on my own. Hundreds of people donated some of their hard-earned money or gave some of their precious spare time to deliver leaflets or knock on doors. These people – and others like them in all parties all over the country – are the unsung heroes and heroines of our politics. They're not 'in it for themselves' – they get involved because they care about their local community and their country and want to change them for the better. This book is dedicated to such people. They deserve a better homage, but it's a start.

Third and most importantly, this book is for anyone who is interested in the gritty coal face of politics. Our political journalists are embedded in Westminster. They produce a huge amount of commentary on the leaders of our political parties, their campaign strategies and key messages – what is sometimes collectively termed the 'air war'. Elections, however, are won and lost on the pavements of only about 100 of the 650 constituencies – places like my constituency of Croydon Central. These places are quite different from SW1. And coverage of what the political parties do in these constituencies – the so-called 'ground war' – is both rarer and sometimes ill-informed.

This book attempts to redress the balance. My aim is to give an insight into what it's like to be an MP defending an ultra-marginal seat. I hope that insight will be of interest to supporters of all parties, even if those who aren't Conservatives will disagree with much of what I was campaigning for.

Some may be interested in understanding why political parties campaign in the way we do. Why do activists bother knocking on people's doors – do they really think a quick conversation is going to change someone's mind? Why do they stand outside polling stations with coloured rosettes on? Some may be interested in the detail of what we did in Croydon Central – the voters we targeted, the messages we employed, the literature we delivered – looking for lessons to employ in their own campaigns. Others still may be interested in how it felt to be in my shoes. What was it like to find myself the subject of an unhelpful story on the front page of a major newspaper? Did the abuse on Twitter bother me? How did I cope with the pressure of knowing my job was on the line? What effect did it have on the rest of my life? It's all here.

In terms of what it's like to do the job, the real divide among MPs isn't between Conservatives and Labour, but between those with safe seats and those whose jobs are on the line at each election. If you're lucky enough to get selected for a safe seat then unless you do something very stupid, or there are major boundary changes or a political earthquake like the one we've seen recently in Scotland, you've got a job for life. General elections aren't about whether you're going to be in the next House of Commons, but whether you're going to be on the government or opposition benches. If you're an MP in a marginal seat, however, your job is on the line every five years. It's a fixed-term contract with a five-year-long job interview to decide if it gets renewed.

And your fate isn't entirely in your own hands. If you do a good job, a few people who wouldn't normally vote for your party will vote for you – what is known as a personal vote. Most votes aren't personal, though; on the whole, people care more about which party gets to run the country than who their local MP is. Some of the nicest yet most frustrating conversations I had during the campaign were with lifelong Labour voters who said, 'I really admire what you have done as our MP, but I'm sorry: I can't vote for a Tory.'

The hard truth is that if the national tide is against your party it doesn't matter how good a job you have done. And sooner or later the national tide *will* be against your party. You may hold your marginal seat at the next election or even the election after that, but one day, however hard you work, you're going to lose.

Marginal-seat MPs cope with this in different ways. A few conclude they're not going to win and give up. Others graft as hard as they can. The rest fluctuate between these two extremes as their party rises and falls in the polls.

Of course, many MPs in safe seats work hard too. They may not be in danger of losing their seats, but they still want to do a good job for their constituents. The good ones also campaign in a nearby marginal seat. However, the average MP in a safe seat inevitably knocks on far fewer doors and delivers far fewer leaflets in their own seat than the average MP in a marginal. As a result, they receive less casework.[1] They're also under less pressure to spend all their time on constituency issues, leaving them with more time to pursue national or international issues they're interested in. In my time as an MP, my total overseas travel has been one day trip to CERN in Switzerland with the Science & Technology Select Committee. It's not that I'm more virtuous than the next MP – I simply can't justify spending a week on a cross-party visit fostering better relations with Taiwan when I could be campaigning in my seat. Representing a marginal seat is a very different job.

Lastly, and selfishly, this book is for me. The twelve months leading up to polling day were incredibly tough. I had to combine being a government minister, an MP, a candidate running for re-election in an ultra-marginal seat and a husband and father. I averaged five hours' sleep a night and most nights I would wake up at least once in a cold sweat over something that hadn't been done or with an idea of something new I could do to improve my chances, which I would quickly scribble down on a pad of paper I kept next to my bed, then try to get back to sleep.

I wasn't just worried about losing my job and with it the chance to change my home town for the better; there were six people working for me whose livelihoods also depended on me winning. It became very difficult to strike anything approaching a sane work/life balance. My wife Karen would often ask, 'Do you have

1 If you knock on people's doors and deliver leaflets, some people will contact you who wouldn't otherwise have done so.

to go to that event?' She was right – I didn't *have* to go and it was highly unlikely that attendance at any one event would ultimately make a difference on polling day. It all adds up, however, and I believed the cumulative effect *could* make the difference. I dreaded losing by a handful of votes and thinking, 'If only I'd worked harder.' So I'd squeeze an extra event into an already crowded diary, produce another leaflet, do six hours' canvassing on Saturday instead of five, waste less time asleep. 'It'll all be over soon,' I'd say to myself. 'Get to polling day and then you can get some rest.' In the event, I've found it very hard to recover. Hopefully, writing this book will be cathartic.

One thing I'm not trying to do is elicit sympathy. There are millions of people in this country with far worse-paid and less secure jobs than me. And as I explain in the first chapter, I applied for this job knowing exactly what it would involve. If you're going to feel sorry for anyone, my Labour opponent Sarah Jones deserves it more – she also worked incredibly hard, only to lose by the skin of her teeth.

Despite what I went through over those twelve months, as far as I am concerned being the MP for the place I've lived virtually my entire life is the best job in the world. Would I go through it all again if I had to? In the words of Ed Miliband, the man to whom I owe so much:

'Hell, yes.'

Prologue

5.45 a.m., Friday 8 May 2015

IN MOST CONSTITUENCIES, the result of the general election has been declared.

The Conservative Party is on course to win significantly more seats than it did in 2010. David Cameron is not only going to continue as Prime Minister, but against all the odds he is going to be able to form a majority Conservative government.

If I can hold my seat, I'm in with a chance of playing a reasonably significant role in that government. In outer London, however, things aren't going so well. On a night when Labour have been doing very badly in nearly every other part of the country, they've gained seats in Brentford, Ealing, Enfield and Ilford. Will mine be next?

In 2010, I won by nearly 3,000 votes. This time, the result is too close to call – so close the votes are being re-counted. Five years of hard work, twelve months of relentless campaigning and now my future depends on whether a handful of votes have been miscounted. I'm not at the count. I can't bear them. I'm at home with my family and a few close friends. The sense of euphoria when the exit poll was announced at 10 p.m. the previous night now seems a lifetime ago.

My mobile phone rings. Everyone in the room goes quiet. The name Ian Parker flashes up on the display. It's my campaign manager. Nervously, I answer. He's phoning with the result: I've won by the tiniest of majorities, just 165 votes. Who cares about the narrowness of the margin? It's a win. This is the moment I've dreamt about for five years.

I should be ecstatic. All I feel, however, is a sense of dull relief. What has this campaign done to me?

Chapter 1

Only myself to blame

Beginnings

LIKE MANY MPs, I got interested in politics when I was quite young.

My parents were Conservative voters, but they weren't members of the party or politically active in any way. My earliest memory of politics intruding on my life is of having to do homework in candlelight because of power cuts caused by strikes. Then, when I was seven, I was diagnosed with lymphatic cancer. The NHS saved my life, but the consultant who was in charge of my treatment ended up emigrating because he was fed up having to cross picket lines to treat his patients. I saw on the news that the Prime Minister, Margaret Thatcher, agreed with me that something needed to be done about all these strikes. She was clearly a very sensible person. I was well on the way to thinking of myself as a Conservative.

My best friends at secondary school shared my interest in politics, but they weren't Conservatives. Rather than join our respective parties, we figured it would be more fun to join the school debating club (it was where all the cool kids hung out...). Likewise, at university I didn't get involved in the Conservative Association, but joined the Cambridge Union Society, a historic debating society with many senior politicians among its former presidents.[2]

The person to thank (or blame, depending on your perspective) for getting me actively involved in politics was my room-mate in my last year at Cambridge, Steve Postlewhite. He was concerned about what I was going to do with my life after I graduated with a degree in theoretical physics. And he was right to be concerned: I knew I didn't want to be a theoretical physicist and I'm pretty sure theoretical physics wasn't all that keen on me either; beyond that, I had no idea. So Steve took it upon himself to find me a job. He selected a hundred random job adverts from the careers library and took them and me to the Mitre pub. He was getting nowhere until he came to an advert for a job in the Conservative Research Department, whatever that was. I didn't immediately reject this one out of hand, which Steve figured was about as positive a reaction as he was going to get, so he dragged me down to the computer room to write a CV and covering letter. They ended up offering me the job and, with nothing else to do and student loans to pay off, I accepted, starting work on 6 September 1993. After three years as a student, a salary of £12,000 a year seemed like riches beyond compare.

2 I think this background in debating has made me a better politician today. In a debating competition you don't get to choose which side you speak on, which means you have to be able to see both sides of every argument. This ability to understand other people's points of view is both crucial if you are trying to shift public opinion and sadly all too rare.

Working in politics

The Research Department turned out to be part of Conservative Central Office, as Conservative Campaign Headquarters (CCHQ) was then called. At the time, it was based at 32 Smith Square in Westminster, a stone's throw from the Houses of Parliament (the building is now the UK headquarters of the European Union).

I was hooked from day one. Within days I was attending meetings with Cabinet ministers and I was being paid to do it.

After a year and a half in the Research Department, I was appointed as special adviser to John Gummer, the then Secretary of State for the Environment. Special advisers, known as spads, are civil servants, but unlike most civil servants, who are obliged to be politically neutral, they are party-political appointments. My job was to provide political advice to the ministers in the Department of the Environment and be the link between their offices and the Conservative Party organisation. It was fascinating and it gave me a great insight into how the machinery of government works. Plus the civil service certainly paid better than the Conservative Party – John Gummer's private secretary was amused to discover that my previous salary was so low that technically I didn't qualify for the lowest point on the spad salary scale.

In May 1997, however, the great British public fired the Conservative government and me along with it. So back to Conservative Central Office I went.

Elected office

Back in the Research Department, my first line manager had been a take-no-prisoners right-winger called Peter Campbell, known as 'Rambo' to his friends.[3] By coincidence, Peter was also from

3 Unlike Rambo, Peter has evolved in his views and he is now very much a moderniser.

Croydon and in 1994 he stood for election to Croydon Council. The ward he was standing in was normally a safe Conservative ward, but John Major's government was so unpopular that nowhere could be regarded as safe. I offered to help out on polling day.

This would be my first experience of grass-roots campaigning and what I assumed would be the well-oiled Conservative Party election machine. After a couple of hours knocking on doors, we went to the home of a party member for something to eat. We were sat down and served a three-course meal, including a roast with all the trimmings and an enormous trifle. There were second, then third portions. It went on for hours. We must have spent half the day trapped at the table, not wanting to offend the catering team who had gone to such lengths to make sure we were well fed. Nevertheless, despite our rather feeble efforts Peter somehow managed to get elected and I developed a taste for local politics (and trifle).

Two and a half years later, I was selected as a council candidate myself in the safe Conservative ward of Woodcote & Coulsdon West. On 7 May 1998 I was elected as a local councillor.

Guinea pig

Although I was now a councillor, I still had my day job. I was back in the Research Department as head of the political section, probably the most enjoyable job I've ever had. My predecessor but one in the role was George Osborne and his predecessor but one was David Cameron, which means either I'm destined for great things or I'm not as talented as them – answers on a postcard.

Every week, I would brief whoever was representing the Conservatives on *Question Time* and *Any Questions?* on the party's position on the stories that had been in the news that week. The best part of the job, though, was helping my boss Danny Finkelstein prepare William Hague for Prime Minister's Questions (PMQs).

The Conservative Party had suffered a terrible defeat and was divided and exhausted after eighteen years in government; William's performances at PMQs were the only thing keeping the show on the road. As well as Danny and I, the prep sessions on Tuesday evenings and Wednesday mornings also involved William's political secretary, George Osborne; his press secretary, Gregor Mackay (sadly no longer with us); and his parliamentary private secretary, David Lidington. I was very clearly the most junior person in the room.

These were the most intellectually challenging meetings I've ever attended – you quickly learnt to open your mouth only if you were sure of your ground and to be prepared to defend your point with both facts and passion. However, they are the closest my experience of politics has yet come to an episode of *The West Wing* – even if the meetings were always held in an office, rather than while walking through mysteriously endless corridors – and it was incredibly satisfying when the line of questioning we settled on worked in the House of Commons. All in all, everything was going very nicely for me.

And then Archie Norman intervened.

William had appointed Archie to reorganise the Conservative Party – indeed, you could say he was appointed to *create* the Conservative Party since legally it didn't exist before his reforms. What people knew as the Conservative Party was a combination of autonomous units: the National Union (a federation of the Conservative associations that existed in each parliamentary constituency), the parliamentary party and Conservative Central Office.

Central Office was divided by a Chinese wall. On one side was the Research Department and the Press Office, both staffed by hungry young graduates learning their trade for a couple of years before moving on. On the other side was the Campaigning Department, which employed people who had trained to become qualified Conservative Party agents and for whom working for the party was therefore a long-term career. Archie wanted to encourage some cross-fertilisation between the two parts of Central Office and I was his guinea pig. He moved me from the Research Department to become head of local government in the Campaigning Department. Suddenly I went from helping to brief William Hague for PMQs to developing a strategy to rebuild the Conservative Party's strength in local government and advising our councillors and activists on how to win council elections.

I wasn't very happy about this at first. Nor were most of my new colleagues, who felt that someone who wasn't a qualified agent shouldn't be taking one of the most senior positions in their department. I couldn't really blame them. It turned out to be a good move, however, both for me personally – I proved to be a better campaign strategist than I had been a policy adviser – and, as others followed in my footsteps, for the party as a whole.

Wannabe MP

If you work for a political party for any length of time, you end up either unable to understand why anyone in their right mind would want to be an MP or fed up with being an adviser and keen to stand for election yourself. You can guess which category I fell into.

Having got onto the national list of people eligible to be selected as a Conservative parliamentary candidate, I started applying to seats. After one failed attempt in Guildford, in 2002 I was selected as the Conservative candidate for Sutton & Cheam. Given that I wasn't going to compete with my friend Andrew Pelling for the vacancy in Croydon Central, Sutton & Cheam was on paper the perfect seat – not too far from home and a marginal, which meant I had a chance of winning.

In practice, it wasn't as perfect as it seemed. Some party members were very unhappy I had been selected, as they made abundantly clear to me and my wife Karen at the end of the selection meeting. And I was soon unhappy too. I discovered I didn't enjoy campaigning in an area I didn't know. When we ran campaigns in Croydon, they were about places I knew or services I used. In Sutton, I didn't have any personal connection with what I was doing. Without that passion for the area, it wasn't the same.

More importantly, though, my father's health began to deteriorate rapidly. He had been suffering from dementia for some time, but his condition now started to get much worse. To win Sutton & Cheam, I needed to be 100 per cent committed to it, but all I really wanted to do was spend my spare time with my family. After about a year, I decided to stand down. It was one of the hardest decisions of my professional life. I was acutely conscious I was letting down the people who had voted for me at the selection meeting. I was also aware that if I threw in the towel here, I might not get another chance at becoming an MP.

Some things are more important than politics, though. I got to spend more time with my dad in the last months of his life. He passed away in early 2005, shortly before the general election.

Learning from Lynton

Nationally, Iain Duncan Smith had replaced William Hague as leader of the party. In the autumn of 2003, he in turn was replaced by Michael Howard. My boss Stephen Gilbert moved on to pastures new and I was appointed director of operations, the most senior member of the party's staff.

It wasn't an easy time. Michael Howard had appointed two co-chairmen of the party to whom I reported, Liam Fox and Maurice Saatchi. On a personal level, they were both a pleasure to work for – committed and full of ideas. Unfortunately, there was no clear demarcation of their responsibilities, leading to days when each would invite you to a meeting about the same issue with the two meetings coming to different conclusions.

To clarify things, Michael appointed Lynton Crosby as campaign director. Lynton had masterminded John Howard's victories in Australia and he made an immediate difference, setting up a clear structure with three deputies: George Bridges, responsible for policy and messaging; George Eustice, responsible for media relations; and me, responsible for our target seat and target voter campaigns.

Lynton had two great strengths. First was his ability to get the senior politicians to agree a strategy and key messages and stick to them. As anyone who has worked in politics will tell you, this is no mean feat. Second was his ability to motivate everyone in CCHQ. Despite the fact that we were heading for a third consecutive defeat, morale in HQ was much better than in 1997 or 2001 and that was almost exclusively down to Lynton. No one who worked on the 2005 campaign will ever forget his daily staff meetings, which combined communicating important information about what we were planning to do over the next few days with raucous team-building exercises like staff of each nationality singing their national anthem and the award of 'tinnies' to junior staffers who had done a great job. It was an object lesson in how strong leadership can maintain morale even in the most stressful and difficult conditions.

What Lynton was not able to do, having been appointed less than seven months before the general election, was to address the underlying problems with the Conservative Party's brand, the things that stopped people who agreed with our critique of the Labour government from voting for us. The result was that although the Labour share of the vote fell by 5.7 percentage points to 35 per cent, which normally wouldn't be enough to win an overall majority, the main beneficiaries were the Liberal Democrats. Our vote share only increased by 0.6 percentage points and Labour won again.

It was scant consolation for another five years of Labour government, but, as I wrote in an academic paper published after the election, we could take some pride from our target seat campaign:

> Unlike in 2001, when we did worst in the seats that we had the best chance of gaining, we got a bigger swing in the Labour-held seats that we were targeting than across the country as a whole ... We can take particular pride in our performance in Conservative/Liberal Democrat marginals. Across the country as a whole, there was a swing of 1.7 per cent from the Conservatives to the Liberal Democrats, but in the Liberal Democrat-held seats we targeted there was a swing of 0.4 per cent from them to us and in the seats we were defending against them a swing of 1.1 per cent from them to us.

One of the target seats where we had outperformed the national swing was Croydon Central, which my friend Andrew Pelling managed to win by just seventy-five votes. I was thrilled for him. The result was a reward for years of dedicated service as a councillor and London Assembly member.

An offer I couldn't refuse

Michael Howard resigned the day after polling day, so my first job post-general election was to run the resulting leadership election.

Once David Cameron was elected, I decided it was time to move on. On one level, this was a strange decision: politically, I was much closer to David than to any of the previous leaders I had worked for. However, apart from a two-year stint as a spad I'd been at CCHQ since 1997 – it was time for a change. So I had a chat with the new party chairman, Francis Maude, and told him I would be leaving at the end of May 2006.

At this point, I had two young children. Karen was understandably alarmed when I went home to tell her I had handed in my notice and didn't know what I was going to do next. 'I'm sure something will turn up,' I reassured her, wondering if something would turn up. Fortunately it did, when I got a call from Michael Ashcroft the very next day.

I'd known Michael since the late 1990s when he'd been the treasurer of the Conservative Party and I'd done some presentations to potential donors with him. David Cameron had recently appointed him as deputy chairman of the party with responsibility for polling and target seats, two areas Michael had a particular expertise in.

In the run-up to the 2005 election, Michael felt that the party's private polling was designed to paint an overly optimistic picture of our prospects – he termed it 'comfort polling'. He also felt we should target fewer seats, accepting that we weren't going to win that election, but putting ourselves in the best possible position to win the next one. He felt so strongly about these two points that he commissioned his own polling to check whether his instincts were right. When this confirmed his fears, he stopped donating to CCHQ and started directly funding the marginal seats he thought we had a chance of winning, in effect running his own target seats campaign. After the election, he published all his research together with his analysis of what the party needed to do to win again in the excellent *Smell the Coffee*.

Michael had heard from Francis that I was leaving and wondered if I might be interested in working for him on the target seat campaign. His offer was appealing on two levels – the opportunity to continue working on election campaigns without having to put up with the internal politics of CCHQ and the opportunity to pay off my mortgage quicker.

Michael only had one question to ask me: could I commit to working for him through to the next election or was I still interested in becoming an MP? I gave him a straight answer: after my experience in Sutton & Cheam, I wasn't interested in applying to be the candidate for somewhere I didn't know. However, in the unlikely event that Andrew Pelling in Croydon Central or Richard Ottaway in Croydon South decided to retire, I would want to apply. He was happy with that, so I accepted his offer.

Michael was a great boss. He had a clear idea what he wanted – to bring his business acumen to the target seats campaign, using polling to identify which seats were winnable and then investing in those seats that most needed help and whose candidates had good business plans. On the flip side, he refused to help candidates who weren't delivering or local parties that were sitting on significant funds they were saving for a 'rainy day'.

He wasn't a micro-manager either. He employed people he was confident would do a good job and once he had explained to them what he wanted he let them get on with it. He wasn't bothered where you did your work or what time of day you did it as long as it was completed on time and to a high standard.

He would occasionally call and ask you to come and meet him wherever he was in the world. I remember one occasion when my phone rang while I was at a family get-together. The conversation went something like this:

MA: Where are you?

GB: I'm at a picnic in the New Forest.

MA: Whereabouts exactly?

GB: A couple of miles west of Brockenhurst. Why? What's up?

Muffled conversation in the background.

MA: There's an airport a few miles to the west of you at Hurn. Can you be there in an hour?

GB: I'm in a T-shirt and a pair of shorts, I don't have a change of clothes or anything else with me.

MA: Don't worry about that, we can buy stuff when you get out here. Just be at the airport in an hour.

So Karen took me to the airport, where she was allowed to drive onto the apron right up to the plane that was waiting for me. If I hadn't been dressed as I was and arrived in a beat-up Vauxhall Zafira, I'd have felt like a Bond villain. I fell asleep during the flight and woke up in what turned out to be Kefalonia. The furthest the Conservative Party had ever sent me was Llandrindod Wells.

Eventually, we had to move back into CCHQ. David Cameron understandably decided that he wanted polling and the target seat campaign run as part of the overall campaign, not a separate operation. Even when we were back there, however, Michael was very effective at protecting us from internal politics.

Whatever's happened since, I'm proud of the work we did together in the run-up to the 2010 election. We ended up winning thirty-four more seats than we would have done on a uniform swing. Had we not done so, Labour would have been the largest party in the 2010–15 parliament and Gordon Brown would almost certainly have continued as Prime Minister.

Decision time

I'd pretty much given up on the idea of being an MP. And then in the autumn of 2007 an opportunity suddenly arose, but in the worst way possible.

I was driving home from work on 18 September when I was called by Mike Fisher, the Conservative leader of Croydon Council. He told me Andrew Pelling had been arrested on suspicion of assaulting his second wife, Lucy.

I was dumbstruck. Andrew was duly suspended from the parliamentary party while the Crown Prosecution Service (CPS) decided whether he would be charged. There was widespread coverage in the local and national media.

Opinion within Croydon Conservatives was mixed. Everyone admired the work Andrew had done as a councillor and London Assembly member. Many party members had known him since he was a teenager and were very close to him. Sympathy from many of our activists, particularly our councillors, was in shorter supply, however. Andrew had tried to continue as leader of the

Conservative group on Croydon Council after his election as MP and, when that failed, had begun to publicly criticise the work of Conservative councillors in increasingly strident terms. Now, some wouldn't be sorry to see him go.

Under enormous personal pressure, Andrew announced that he would not be standing for re-election. The party quickly launched a process to select a new candidate. Almost immediately, people started ringing me encouraging me to apply.

It was decision time.

I knew what I would be letting myself in for. Andrew had won Croydon Central by about enough voters to fill one double decker bus. The constituency boundaries were due to change at the next election in a way that favoured Labour (if the 2005 election had been fought on the revised boundaries, Andrew would not have won). I also suspected that if Andrew wasn't charged he would change his mind about not wanting to be an MP anymore – after all, it was his life's ambition. If that happened, he might stand against our candidate as an independent, making the seat even more difficult to win.

And even if I did win, would I be able to go on holding the seat? Like many outer London boroughs, Croydon's black and minority ethnic population was increasing and it was becoming more deprived. Both of these changes tended to favour Labour. Karen certainly thought I should pass on the opportunity and try to get selected for the safe Conservative seat of Croydon South at some point in the future when Richard Ottaway stood down.

If I had learnt anything from my time in politics, however, it was to take your opportunity when it comes. There were only two things I needed to check. First, Andrew was a friend. There was no way I was putting my name forward if there was any chance he could still be the candidate. What if he wasn't charged and he changed his mind and decided he wanted to carry on – could he be reinstated? I was advised by both the Chief Whip, Patrick McLoughlin, and the head of the Candidates Department at CCHQ, Gareth Fox, that this was impossible now that the process of selecting a new candidate was underway. If Andrew wasn't charged and changed his mind about not wanting to be an MP anymore, he would be given the whip back and allowed to apply for other seats, but he wouldn't be our candidate in Croydon Central.

Second, I needed to speak to Michael Ashcroft and get his permission. When he had offered me a job, we'd agreed that the two seats I could apply for were Croydon Central or Croydon South, but at the time it looked very unlikely that there would be a vacancy in either of them. How would he feel now that it had come to pass? He was as good as his word – I could apply for the seat and continue working for him.

Having checked that Andrew couldn't be reinstated and got Michael's permission, I put my name forward along with over a hundred other people. On 13 February 2008, after three rounds of interviews, I was selected as the Conservative candidate for the place where I had grown up. I told the assembled throng: 'The campaign starts today – well, on Monday actually, as I'm taking Karen to New York for the weekend as a Valentine's present.'

I had a better sense of priorities in those days.

Blood, sweat and tears

The campaign that followed soon turned out to be just as bad as I feared.

The CPS decided not to press charges against Andrew. He was very angry that the Conservative Party wouldn't reinstate him as its candidate and began to prepare to stand against me as an independent.

I could understand his anger. It seemed clear to me from the response we were getting on the doorstep, though, that there was no chance of him winning as an independent. People thought he was a good MP and there was some sympathy for him (although a few had seen the media coverage of his arrest and concluded that he was guilty – a clear example of the reputational damage that premature coverage of such cases can do). Most people, however, were focused on who they wanted to run the country, not who they wanted as their MP. At most, our forecasts suggested he might get several thousand votes. That was nowhere near enough to win, but quite enough, if those votes came from people who normally voted Conservative, to gift victory to Labour. Maybe he was so angry that's what he wanted or maybe his anger was clouding his judgement.

We thought long and hard about how to respond to the threat of him standing as an independent and came up with a four-point plan:

1. Despite the clear signs that he was going to stand, we wouldn't expel him from the party until he actually announced his candidacy. We wanted him to stay: if he left, it would be his decision.

2. Andrew had been a good MP. If he did stand, we wouldn't deny this. To try to do so would only make us look silly and further alienate those who were sympathetic to him.

3. We would, however, explain how we had ended up in this position and point out that Andrew was telling Conservative voters he was only standing as an independent because the Conservative Party wouldn't have him, while telling people who were not Conservatives that he was a genuine independent who wouldn't rejoin the Conservative Party even if it begged him to do so.

4. Most importantly, we would make it clear to anyone who wanted a change of government that voting for Andrew wouldn't achieve that. As I said in my statement when he finally announced he was standing, just over five weeks before polling day, it would 'simply

split the anti-Labour vote and risks getting you a Labour MP and five more years of Gordon Brown'.

If having a close friend leave the party to run against me wasn't hard enough, just three days later on 2 April my campaign manager, Lindsay Frost, tragically died.

Lindsay had applied to be our candidate for Croydon Central. I wouldn't have blamed him if he'd said, 'If they don't want me as their candidate, I'm not doing all the leg-work for someone else.' That's how most people would have reacted. Lindsay wasn't most people, though. He devoted the last twenty-five months of his life to trying to get me elected, missing only one canvass session in all that time. And he wasn't just committed: at each session he lifted everyone present with his tremendous gift for making the arduous work of knocking on thousands of doors fun. Each Easter, our core activists go out for a curry to remember a friend who was taken from us too soon. Rest in peace, mate.

At the end of a hard campaign, the count was held at my old school, Trinity. When it was announced that I had won, the school motto, '*Vincit qui patitur*' – 'He who endures conquers' – seemed very apt. Even in victory, though, there was sadness. Sadness for Lindsay, who had played such an integral role in the campaign, but wasn't there to witness its success. And sadness as I saw my mum in the audience and knew we were both thinking of Dad and how much this night would have meant to him.

Despite everything that had happened, I also felt for Andrew. He wasn't there for the declaration – he left well before I arrived, shortly after the first boxes were opened and he realised he'd come a distant third. I tried to offer an olive branch in my victory speech, expressing both my regret that his years of service should end acrimoniously and my belief that people had voted for me because they wanted a change of government, not because they thought I would make a better MP.

Alas the olive branch didn't work: shortly after the election, Andrew joined the Labour Party. He is now a Labour councillor for a ward in Croydon South. It is a sad story from which no one emerges with much credit.

The first decision I took as an MP was to take my agent and the chairman of my local party to Daisy's café on the Lower Addiscombe Road for a fry-up. While we were tucking in, a couple of guys came in. They recognised me and offered their congratulations. As I went to pay, one of them looked up and said, 'That had better not be going on expenses.'

Welcome to life as an MP.

Signs of trouble to come

Proud as I was to be an MP, the result was a clear warning of trouble to come:

Barwell, Gavin (Conservative)	19,657 votes	ELECTED
Ryan, Gerry (Labour)	16,688 votes	
Lambell, Peter (Liberal Democrat)	6,553 votes	
Pelling, Andrew (Independent)	3,239 votes	
Le May, Cliff (BNP)	1,448 votes	
Atkinson, Ralph (UKIP)	997 votes	
Golberg, Bernice (Green)	581 votes	
Gitau, James (Christian Party)	264 votes	
Cartwright, John (MRLP*)	192 votes	
Castle, Michael (Independent)	138 votes	

* Monster Raving Loony Party.

There had been a swing from Labour to the Conservatives of 3.4 per cent, significantly smaller than the national swing of 5 per cent. The key question was: where had Andrew's 3,239 votes come from? If they were mainly from former Conservatives, things were better than they appeared. If not, however – if the swing was smaller because Croydon was changing demographically – I was going to have a real fight on my hands in 2015.

There was no point complaining. I had applied for this job knowing – probably better than anybody – what was involved in trying to hold a marginal seat and knowing Croydon and the demographic change it was experiencing.

I really only had myself to blame.

Chapter 2

Up the creek

As the 2010–15 parliament unfolded, two changes in the national political landscape increased the scale of the challenge I faced. First, the Liberal Democrat vote collapsed. Nationally, the polls suggested that their vote share was down from 23 per cent at the 2010 general election to about 8 per cent, with Labour the main beneficiary of their collapse. In parliamentary by-elections and local government elections in those parts of the country where the Lib Dems had no elected representatives and therefore little organisation on the ground, the collapse was even more dramatic. Croydon was just such a place. Second, UKIP was on the rise. Their vote share was up from just 3 per cent at the 2010 general election to the mid-teens and they appeared to be drawing much, though by no means all, of their support from former Conservatives.

In the first three years of the parliament, we only had one election in Croydon – the 2012 London Mayor and Assembly election. Because this was dominated by a personal contest – Boris versus Ken round two – it wasn't a great predictor of our prospects in a general election. The 2014 council elections would give us a much better insight.

A tale of five wards

The borough of Croydon has three parliamentary constituencies, each made up of eight council wards. All but two of these wards elect three councillors each; Fieldway and New Addington are smaller and only elect two councillors each. This gives a total of seventy councillors.

The last council elections had been held on the same day as the 2010 general election, and we had won thirty-seven of the seats, with Labour winning the other thirty-three. However, this tight overall result masked the fact that most wards were either strongly Conservative or strongly Labour.

Labour won all twenty-four seats in Croydon North and we had little chance of gaining any of them. We won all twenty-four seats in Croydon South and with the exception of the three seats in Waddon Labour had little chance of gaining any of them. Only in my constituency of Croydon Central were several wards close contests. New Addington was so marginal that it elected one Conservative councillor and one Labour councillor; we won Ashburton and Fairfield, but not by enough to be certain of holding them; and likewise Labour won Addiscombe, but not by enough to be certain of holding it.

The election would therefore be decided in just five of the twenty-four wards: Addiscombe, Ashburton, Fairfield, New Addington and Waddon.

A campaign of two halves

Our ground war in these five wards – the delivery of literature and door-to-door canvassing to identify potential Conservative supporters – was co-ordinated by Phil Thomas. Phil was a gifted and incredibly committed grass-roots campaigner (when he holidays in the US he often contacts the local Republican Party office to see if they want any help). He appointed campaign managers in each ward. I was keen to repay the help I had received from our councillors and I obviously had a personal interest in us getting good results in Croydon Central, so I volunteered to run the campaign in Addiscombe. We were all agreed that the main focus should be on Addiscombe, New Addington and Waddon, with a watching brief on Ashburton and Fairfield in case Labour targeted them. As usual, Tim Pollard, deputy leader of the Conservative group, did a great job designing all the literature. These elements of the campaign worked well – we more than matched Labour in the delivery of literature and the canvass results looked OK.

The air war, which was ultimately the responsibility of the leadership of the Conservative group, was another story.

Labour published a detailed manifesto entitled: 'Ambitious for Croydon'. We never published one, just some pledges on our election leaflets. We were all agreed that our key message should be on council tax, contrasting our record of reducing it in real terms with Labour's record of more than doubling it when they last ran the council. However, Labour came up with an effective, if rather revealing, rebuttal. They didn't try to deny that they wanted to put up council tax. They simply pointed out than under a law passed by the Conservative government any significant increase would need to be put to the electorate in a referendum. No one need worry about them putting up council tax bills, they said, because the electorate would never let them get away with it.

As well as failing to produce a manifesto, we also made virtually no effort to find new candidates. This was a mistake for several reasons. All council groups need an injection of fresh talent every four years. Given the diversity of Croydon, the Conservative group particularly needed more councillors from black and minority ethnic communities – especially the black community – if it was to reflect the town we aspired to serve. And our prospects of winning marginal wards would have been significantly enhanced if we had found candidates who had strong personal votes in those wards.

In Addiscombe, I tried to address these failings. We produced a detailed manifesto for the ward focusing on safety, cleanliness, regeneration of the district centre, better access to East Croydon station and the protection of the area from overdevelopment. And I worked hard to find new potential candidates. The local party ended up selecting three of the people I found: Partha Chatterjee, David Harmes and Lisa Terry. All three lived in the ward, and together they were a well-balanced team.

We also tried to ensure that the information we gathered about people's voting intentions was as accurate as possible. Some Conservative supporters were thinking of voting UKIP, but appeared reluctant to admit to it unless specifically asked. If we weren't precise with our canvassing, we were therefore in danger of getting a misleading impression of how we were doing. In hindsight, this is what happened in some of our other target wards, but in Addiscombe we got more accurate data because we invested time at the outset in training our canvassers.

Warning signs

The first moment in a campaign when you get a sense of how people have actually voted (as opposed to how they say they are going to vote) is about ten days before polling day when council officers start opening returned postal ballot papers to verify them. They don't count how many votes each candidate receives, just check that the votes are valid, ensuring that the signature and date of birth match those originally provided by the elector when they requested a postal vote, to speed up the count on the night. However, representatives of each candidate are allowed to scrutinise the process and it's possible to see some ballot papers and so get a feel for how you're doing.

On this occasion, it was clear we were in trouble. We looked fine in Fairfield, but everywhere else things were not as good as we had hoped. We were ahead in Ashburton and Waddon, but not by enough to feel comfortable. We were behind in Addiscombe. And we were well behind in New Addington, where UKIP were polling very strongly.

This is always the most difficult moment in a council election campaign. Do you trust this information enough to redirect manpower away from the wards you feel are already won or lost and into the ones you think are still up for grabs? And even if you do, is it fair to abandon a councillor who has worked hard for the last four years (which is what giving up on New Addington would have meant)? We couldn't agree, so we carried on spreading our resources over five wards when the data from the postal vote openings showed that only three were in the balance and events took their course.

A night to forget

I don't like counts even when we're winning. You arrive exhausted, having spent the previous twelve hours pounding the streets. Unless it's incredibly close, you quickly get an idea whether you have won or lost, but it then takes hours to get the final result.

In this case, it was clear from very early on in the night that we had lost. We won Fairfield, where remarkably there was a swing to us since 2010, but that was the only bright spot. In Addiscombe, we did as well as in 2010 – not a bad result given that nationally the polls were showing a clear swing to Labour, but not good enough to gain any of the three seats. We lost all three of the other target wards with strong swings to Labour, agonisingly losing the third seat in Ashburton by just eight votes.

The loss of Ashburton was a particular blow. Labour had never won this ward before. In Addiscombe, New Addington and Waddon we had done all we could, but the Ashburton campaign had been under-resourced. The team there had known Labour were working hard, but it was only on polling day, when they were swamped with Labour activists, that they pressed the panic button and by then it was too late. In hindsight, I should have spent my time there, not in Addiscombe.

Although our campaign hadn't been perfect, the real reasons for our defeat weren't local; they were those two changes in the national political landscape. The UKIP share of the vote had ballooned from 3 per cent in 2010 to 15.5 per cent and the Liberal Democrat share of the vote had collapsed from 18.8 per cent in 2010 to 5.5 per cent – and even more dramatically in some of the target wards. Labour deserved credit for maximising this squeeze, but if it were not for the Liberal Democrats' problems it is very unlikely they would have won – there was very little evidence of voters switching directly from Conservative to Labour.

I felt a huge amount of sympathy for friends like Adam Kellett and Tony Pearson who had lost their seats; for candidates like David, Lisa and Partha in Addiscombe who had worked so hard only to fall just short; and for our senior councillors, who had done a good job turning round the fortunes of our town only to lose because of changes in the national political landscape.

Politics can be a tough game sometimes. Some of our councillors had given up their jobs to run the council and now urgently needed to find new ones. Unlike MPs, who receive payments if they lose their seats, or people doing a normal job, who are at least eligible for statutory redundancy, councillors don't receive a penny if they lose.

A sense of foreboding

On a selfish level, the results were also a grim portent for my prospects of holding my parliamentary seat in a year's time. As the map below shows, Labour had won five of the eight wards that made up my constituency; we had only won three. If you added up the results, Labour had won 35.3 per cent of the vote to our 33.5 per cent. That represented a swing to Labour of 4.4 per cent since 2010, more than enough for them to defeat me if it was repeated in twelve months' time.

And it wasn't just the raw numbers. Some of our defeated candidates were bound to give up on local politics, weakening our organisation in key parts of the constituency, while Labour's new councillors would be working hard to strengthen their organisation. The only possible silver lining to the result was that the new Labour-controlled council might not do a very good job, giving me something to attack – but that was hardly something to look forward to because it would be bad news for the town.

The result was also bound to be noticed by Labour HQ. Croydon Central was one of their target seats, but hadn't yet received a lot of national support. With these results, that would surely change. And that would put me at a significant disadvantage because we weren't one of the Conservative Party's target seats.

If Labour were targeting Croydon Central, why, you might ask, weren't the Conservatives doing the same? The answer is that the two parties were starting from very different positions. Labour had one of their worst ever results in 2010. They therefore felt it was safe to assume they would hold all the seats they already had in England and Wales[4] (Scotland was clearly a very different kettle of fish) and concentrate all their efforts on seats they needed to gain in order to win an overall majority. The Conservative Party, on the other hand, had done reasonably well in 2010. We had to gain some extra seats if we were to win an overall majority, though nowhere near as many as Labour, but we also needed to defend the seats we had only just won in 2010.

There is a limit on how many seats you can target – if you try to target too many, you end up spreading your resources so thinly that they make no difference. Labour couldn't target all the seats it needed to win an overall majority *and* defend seats it only just won in 2010; the Conservatives couldn't defend all the seats Labour were

4 Remarkably, this turned out to be false – they ended up losing some seats to us – but given their lead in the opinion polls a couple of years before polling day, it was a reasonable assumption to make at the time.

attacking *and* target the extra seats we needed to win an overall majority. The result was that the two target seat lists didn't overlap – Labour were attacking some Conservative seats like Croydon Central that CCHQ considered to be safe and we were attacking some Labour seats that Labour HQ considered to be safe.

Publicly, I put a brave face on the council election results, telling the media:

> I need to secure a swing of just under 1 per cent over the next year – perfectly doable (indeed quite a few voters have said to us over the last few weeks that they would be voting UKIP this year, but would back me next year), but by no means inevitable. Beneath the very disappointing headline result, there were some grounds for optimism in some wards. In Addiscombe and Fairfield, we actually increased our share of the vote compared with 2010, a remarkable achievement.

The truth, however, was that I was some way up a well-known creek.

Chapter 3

Designing a paddle

I NEEDED A PADDLE and I needed one quick.

My golden rule of campaigning is to focus on the things you can influence and not worry about other stuff. There was nothing I could do to stop the Liberal Democrat vote share collapsing and much of it going to Labour. As for the national Labour Party, they were hardly going to refrain from putting significant resources into my seat even if I asked them really, really nicely.

Given that Labour were going to gain votes from the Liberal Democrats and work the seat harder than they had in 2010, it was almost certain that they would get as many votes as I did in 2010, possibly slightly more. I therefore needed a strategy that would deliver a couple of thousand more votes than I got in 2010. That sounds simple, but achieving it after the tough decisions we had taken over the previous five years and with UKIP appealing to our core vote would be anything but.

So how to do it?

Let Barwell be Barwell

My second golden rule of campaigning (I have a lot of golden rules – there's even one about how many rules there are allowed to be) is to be true to yourself.

This book is full of things I did to try to get more people to vote for me, but the one thing I was never prepared to do was pretend to be something I'm not. What's the point in being an MP if you're not going to stand up for what you believe in? In any case, voters are very good at spotting authenticity – if you're just pretending to believe in something, you're unlikely to convince anyone.

I voted for same-sex marriage (with protection for religious groups that don't want to conduct such marriages) even though I knew it was likely to cost me votes because I believe in equality and in freedom of religion. I helped set up a cross-party group called Migration Matters to make the case for immigration, even though I knew many of my constituents weren't very keen on it, because although I shared their concern about numbers I believe that at the right level immigration is good for our country and I despise the way some people try to blame migrants for all our problems.

As you probably spotted from the previous paragraph, I'm a liberal Conservative. From an electoral point of view, that had some disadvantages. Someone like John Redwood would have been much better placed than me to appeal to disillusioned Conservatives who were tempted to vote UKIP. However, it also had its advantages. My views put me firmly in the centre ground in my constituency, making me a much harder target for Labour to attack. I campaigned for a living wage, for action to tackle tax dodgers and for help for the world's poorest. I talked about full employment and educational equality and how Conservative policies were bringing us closer to these goals. If my Labour opponent, Sarah Jones, wanted to differentiate herself from me, she would have to position herself well to the left.

Framing the choice

The key strategic decision I needed to take was what my core message should be.

Lynton Crosby always says a campaign should 'frame the choice' – define in simple terms what the election is about. The choice you present to voters must resonate. If they don't agree with your characterisation of what the election is about, it doesn't matter how many doors you knock or leaflets you drop, you're not going to win. In 2001, most voters agreed with William Hague that we should keep the pound, but they didn't agree that the future of the pound was the most important issue at that election – not least because Labour had promised a separate referendum if they ever decided we should join the euro.

As well as resonating, the choice you present must make people more likely to vote for you. In February 1974, most voters agreed with Edward Heath that the election was about who could govern Britain and deal with the trade unions, but their answer to that question was, 'Not you.'

So what should my message be? We knew from published national opinion polling that although the electorate marginally preferred a Labour government to a Conservative one, they strongly preferred David Cameron to Ed Miliband. They weren't wildly enthusiastic about any politician, but faced with a choice between the two of them – which is what they would ultimately face on polling day – David won by about two to one. Polling also showed that we had a strong lead on who people trusted to manage the economy. And finally, we knew from our local surveys that most people thought I had done a good job as their MP.

So my core message would be, 'If you want David Cameron, not Ed Miliband, running the country and managing our economy; and you want to keep Gavin Barwell as our hard-working, local MP, vote Conservative on 7 May.'

Running on my record

As well as a core message, I would need detailed messages on a whole range of issues – the regeneration of central Croydon, the rail service to London, our local NHS, school standards, immigration, you name it.

Unlike my Labour opponent, who was essentially a blank canvas, I had been the MP for five years so I had a record to run on. Among other things, I had secured funding to rebuild our town after the riots, helped to bring Westfield and Hammerson to Croydon to redevelop our shopping centre, taken the Mental Health Discrimination Act through Parliament, got funding for new school places and helped introduce Lillian's Law to tackle drug-driving. This record was a key part of my message.

A man with a plan

However, keen as I was to tell everyone what a good job I'd done, elections are more about what you're going to do in the future. Rather than resting on my laurels, I needed to communicate what I would do for the next five years if I was re-elected.

One of our mistakes in the council elections had been our failure to produce a local manifesto. It allowed Labour to portray us as having no vision for the future. I was determined not to repeat that error. This time, I would set the agenda by developing and publishing a comprehensive vision for Croydon and then see if Labour could produce something as detailed.

Rebutting Labour's core message

Labour wanted to frame the election as a choice about the future of the NHS, suggesting it wasn't safe in our hands.

The NHS saved my life as a child and gave outstanding care to my dad at the end of his life. My wife works for it – she's a speech and language therapist working with children in schools in Shirley and Woodside and at a specialist unit in New Addington, all of which are in my constituency.[5] As an MP, I had voted for increases in the NHS budget, got Croydon a fairer share of that budget and was campaigning to get a new accident and emergency department at our local hospital. I wasn't going to let anyone question my commitment to one of the best things about Britain.

How to respond to my Labour opponent?

Another key decision any campaign needs to take is how to respond to your main opponent – in my case, Labour's Sarah Jones.

I've known Sarah (and the Green Party candidate, Esther Sutton) since I was sixteen years old – they were both friends of my first girlfriend, which in itself probably says something about the narrow section of society from which political parties draw their candidates. We'd seen each other every now and then over the years. I didn't know her well enough to call her a friend, but some of my best friends were close to her and her mum and I were fellow governors of a local charity.

These personal connections did make a bit of a difference – there were a couple of occasions during the campaign when I responded differently to her than I would have done to someone I didn't know. Some of you may think that reflects well on me;

---

5 She's often asked if she's related to Gavin Barwell. When she replies that I'm her husband, she either gets told how wonderful I am – an opinion she doesn't always share – or there's an awkward silence.

others that it shows I lack the killer instinct necessary to succeed in politics. I'm still not sure.

When planning how we should to respond to her, we reflected on my experience of running against a sitting MP in 2010. It isn't easy. As a new candidate, you start as an unknown, whereas the MP has had years to build name recognition, and it's much easier for the incumbent to get in the local papers. If Sarah criticised me and I responded, the papers would be more likely to run the story. If I criticised her, the papers would go to her for a response. In both cases, I would be helping her build name recognition. So we decided that the guiding principle should be to ignore her and focus on communicating our message.

There were only two exceptions to this principle. The first was if she made a real gaffe, in which case I *would* criticise her. This happened on two occasions. The most serious of these was after an illegal rave in a building next to East Croydon station on 14 June 2014. This caused major damage to the building, disrupted public transport and the lives of people living nearby and led to several people being injured, one of whom tragically died two days later.

I visited the site early the next morning and called for those responsible for organising the event to 'face the full force of the law'. Sarah – admittedly before the young man had died, but also before she had visited the site to see the damage for herself and speak to local residents – posted on Facebook that I was 'too macho' and that 'youth is about exploration, pushing boundaries, seeking out fun and moulding your personality'. This seemed to me to be a spectacularly ill-judged response from someone seeking to represent a town that had been scarred by rioting three years earlier.

Sarah is not daft and I suspect she quickly regretted saying that. If so, she should have corrected the statement and I would have left the matter there. For whatever reason she never did so, allowing me to question whether she was soft on crime.

The second error she made was at a public meeting she had organised to discuss housing where she said, 'We need to be brave and build in places people might not want us to.' When challenged, she wouldn't explain which places she had in mind, so I was able to highlight this quote in parts of the constituency where there were greenfield sites that developers were looking to build on.

The second exception to the policy of ignoring Sarah was if she came up with a good idea, in which case I would happily and vocally support what she was saying. As things turned out, her campaign generally stuck to repeating Labour's national messages rather than campaigning on local issues, so this only happened once. In October 2014, she and Steve Reed, the Labour MP for Croydon North, launched a campaign to move East and West Croydon stations from zone 5 to zone 4.

This was a great idea. It would save those of my constituents who bought an annual Travelcard for journeys into central London over £300 a year and it had been done before in Stratford, so it was potentially achievable. I made it clear that I supported this campaign and would do everything I could to make it happen. This was both the right thing to do and good politics because it blunted it as an issue during the campaign.

Target voters

Once we had agreed my message, the next step was to identify which voters to target.

Some people would vote Conservative even if we never knocked on their door or delivered leaflets to them. Some would vote Labour, UKIP, Liberal Democrat or Green no matter how hard we tried to persuade them otherwise. Some wouldn't vote at all. We needed to concentrate our efforts on the people who were likely to vote, had yet to make up their minds how they were going to do so and might be persuaded to vote for me. They were the people who would determine whether I won or lost.

We settled on four groups:

1. disillusioned Conservatives who were tempted to vote UKIP;
2. Liberal Democrat supporters who preferred us to Labour;
3. people who were undecided but preferred David Cameron to Ed Miliband; and
4. people who were undecided, had no preference between David Cameron and Ed Miliband but thought I was a good local MP.

The last group were the toughest to win over because many of them had never voted Conservative before.

My core message would resonate with all four of these groups to some extent, but ideally it needed tailoring to best appeal to each group. With the first group, the focus needed to be on the fact that they would only get an in/out referendum on our membership of the EU if David Cameron was Prime Minister. With the second and third groups, the focus needed to be on David Cameron, not me. With the last group, it was all about me (so at least I got to feel like the main man a quarter of the time).

With disillusioned Conservatives who were tempted to vote UKIP, we also needed to communicate the fact that UKIP had no chance of winning Croydon Central. If people who were normally Conservative supporters voted for them, it would simply help Labour win.

It proved surprisingly difficult to convince people of this. Most people are friendly with people from a similar demographic background to them. UKIP were doing very well among a few demographic groups, but had very little support outside those groups. As a result, when you found someone who was normally Conservative but was tempted to vote UKIP this time and told them UKIP had no chance of winning, they would often reply, 'But all my friends are voting for them.'

We tried reminding such people what had happened in the council elections the year before. UKIP had told people that if they voted UKIP, they would get UKIP. Over 15 per cent of the electorate had done so, but not a single UKIP councillor had been elected. Instead, Labour gained seven seats and control of Croydon Council. People had voted UKIP, but they'd got Labour. This line worked with some people, but by no means everyone.

When the first Ashcroft poll was published (about which more later), we tried using that to show people that UKIP couldn't win. That proved even less effective than referring to the results of the council elections. Lots of people said they didn't trust polls – with some justification, as it turned out.

In the end, we found the answer at Ladbrokes. Far and away our most effective line was something like: 'UKIP can't win here. Don't believe me – I'm clearly biased. When I've gone, go and check the odds the bookies are offering. We and Labour are virtually neck and neck and UKIP are 100–1 outsiders. Do you really think the bookies have got it that wrong?' In the last few weeks of the campaign, my UKIP opponent, Peter Staveley, admitted that the best he could do was come third. This was a godsend and we started to use his words alongside the bookies' odds.

We also needed to convince Liberal Democrat supporters who preferred us to Labour that their party had no chance of winning Croydon Central. Given all the national media coverage about the collapse in the Lib Dem vote, that wasn't so difficult.

Finally, we had to convince all our target voters that their vote might make the difference. This message was particularly important for people who wanted to keep me as their MP, but had never voted Conservative before. We had to convince these people that if they didn't vote for me there was every chance I would no longer be their MP.

In a seat as marginal as Croydon Central, you'd think people wouldn't need much convincing that their vote might make the difference, but that was not the case. Although the constituency as a whole is marginal, it is highly polarised with some strong Conservative areas and some strong Labour areas. When your street is full of posters for one party, it's hard to believe there's much of a battle going on. Many people we talked to were genuinely surprised to learn that they were living in an ultra-marginal seat.

So I now had a core message and I'd identified key target voter groups, with slight variations in the message depending on the target group I was talking to. To deliver these messages we needed to identify which voters were in each group. This would require far more accurate canvassing than we had ever managed before. I describe how we tried to achieve that in Chapter 6.

Building support among Croydon's diverse communities

The proportion of my electorate from black and minority ethnic (BME) communities[6] is increasing rapidly. At the time of the 2001 census, just over 71 per cent of Croydon Central's population described themselves as 'white British'; ten years later, that had fallen to just over 54 per cent.[7]

Historically, electors from these communities have been much less likely to vote Conservative than white British electors (for good reason – in the past, some Conservative politicians were clearly

6 Note the use of the word 'communities'. Many people make the mistake of talking about 'the BME community' or 'the black community', treating people whose grandparents came here from Jamaica as part of the same community as a family that recently arrived from Somalia.

7 Note that the census figures are for the percentage of the population that is white British, not the percentage of the electorate. The former will be lower than the latter, both because a higher proportion of the BME population is under the age of eighteen and therefore not eligible to vote and because some non-'white British' adults are not eligible to vote in general elections – for example, EU citizens from countries other than Ireland.

hostile to them and their families settling in Britain). According to the Ethnic Minority British Election Study published by the Runnymede Trust, the Conservative Party got 16 per cent of the BME vote in the 2010 general election (ranging from 24 per cent of the British Indian vote to 6 per cent of the British Black African vote), compared with 37 per cent of the white vote.

With such a large BME population in Croydon Central, I needed to do better than the national party. And with many electors from these communities having strong conservative values there was plenty of potential to do so. It was going to take time, though.

The reasons people from BME communities were much less likely to vote Conservative were deep-seated. Turning up at a community event or on someone's doorstep and explaining that the Conservative Party had changed wasn't going to convince people to change the habits of a lifetime. It was going to take years of work – perhaps more than five years – to overturn historic perceptions of the party.

I started doing this work as soon as I was selected as a candidate back in 2008, not only for the obvious reason that I wanted people to vote for me, but also as a matter of principle: I believe that the Conservative Party must be for people of all backgrounds who believe in our values, not just for well-off white people. I attended community events, visited places of worship and most importantly campaigned on issues that affect particular communities in my constituency. Whatever our faith or the colour of our skin, I find that people basically want the same things – a secure job to provide for their family, good schools for their kids, an NHS they can rely on and a safe neighbourhood to live in. Beyond these bare necessities, however, there are issues that you're much more likely to care about if you're from a particular community.

In the past, the Conservative Party had a tin ear for such issues, but thankfully that was beginning to change. George Osborne announced changes to Labour's unfair airline passenger duty, under which people flying to the Caribbean had to pay more tax than people on a longer, more polluting flight to Los Angeles (bizarrely, the amount of tax you paid was based on the distance from London to the capital of the country you were flying to, not the actual distance you were travelling). The Prime Minister visited the north of Sri Lanka to draw attention to the need for an independent investigation into war crimes during the recent conflict. And one of my proudest moments as an MP was being in the House of Commons when Theresa May announced reforms to stop-and-search. Her action was in clear contrast to the failure of a previous Conservative government to set up a public inquiry into the murder of Stephen Lawrence and concerns among black communities about institutional racism in our police forces.

There was a limit to the progress we could make in five years. However, I was doing everything I could to demonstrate that I was the MP for all of Croydon Central's diverse communities and to explain how the Conservative Party's attitudes to race and diversity were changing. In addition to the specific target voter groups we had identified, we therefore decided to devote some resources to getting these messages to Croydon Central's BME communities.

I'm backing Barwell

I now had a message and a clear sense of who I was trying to communicate it to. The next step was to identify the messenger.

Voters are used to politicians telling them how good they are. They're much more likely to be convinced by a third party who they know. We therefore decided to try to find people throughout the constituency who would endorse me. This was a lot to ask – for many people, how they vote is a private matter, not something they advertise – but we believed it might make the difference with electors who were still undecided.

We used endorsements during the campaign launch and in

the run-up to polling day. In particular, we worked hard to find people who would write an endorsement letter to their neighbours. As I'll go on to describe, these efforts landed me on the front page of the *Evening Standard*, which was the worst moment of the campaign. If I had to fight the whole campaign again, however, I'd put even more effort into recruiting people to write these letters (although I'd take more care about how I did it) – they definitely worked.

Like to get to know me well?

If I was going to maximise my personal vote – people who were voting for me, not the Conservative Party – I needed as many of my constituents as possible to get to know me as a person, so that I was no longer just 'the Conservative Party candidate'.

Putting a leaflet through someone's door doesn't achieve this. Nor, in all but a handful of cases, does knocking on their door and having a brief conversation. I produced a regular email bulletin, which certainly helped, but nothing beats spending an hour or two with people. We tried a number of different formats, including both public meetings about a particular issue and house meetings, where a supporter would invite their neighbours round to meet me and chat about the local area over a cup of coffee or, if I was in luck, a glass of wine. However, the former tended to attract the same people whatever the subject and we struggled to find enough people willing to host the latter.

Ironically, the thing that worked best was nothing to do with the campaign: it was my decision to give guided tours of the Palace of Westminster to groups of my constituents. These tours allowed over 2,000 of my constituents to meet me and get a sense of my passion for the job I do. Although there was nothing party-political about them, I believe they did more to change how people voted than anything else I did.

Shock and awe

The council election campaign had left us bruised and battered. Labour hadn't just beaten us, they had out-campaigned us on the ground, particularly on polling day. Their confidence was sky high, ours was at rock bottom.

I felt it was important to turn that around quickly, to show Labour that this was going to be a much tougher fight than the council elections had been and to convince our own activists that this was going to be a very different campaign with a very different outcome. We needed a bit of shock and awe.

This took several different forms. We were out canvassing again just five weeks after the council elections and in large numbers. We were determined to deliver more literature than Labour. Whenever they made a false claim, we would challenge it. And as a statement of intent, we organised what must be the glitziest launch of an individual constituency campaign British politics has ever seen.

Help! I need some bodies

To get accurate voting intention information for every elector in the constituency and deliver more literature than Labour, we would require an army of volunteers. The story of how we set about recruiting one is for the next chapter.

Money, money, money

And there was one final element to the strategy. Doing all these things would cost a lot of money. We needed to raise it and raise it fast.

Credit where credit's due

I developed this strategy with the help of six people to whom I owe more than I can put into words. They are:

Ian Parker, my campaign manager. Ian is quite simply one of the most loyal, hard-working people I have had the privilege to meet. He's not a huge fan of modern technology, though – he's still using the BlueChip system, which was developed in the late 1980s, to store Croydon Conservatives' membership records. He's also yet to attend a social event at which he feels selling raffle tickets to raise funds for the party is inappropriate behaviour.

Jason Cummings, Ian's assistant. Jason was our data expert and also a meticulous organiser of canvassing sessions. He was in regular demand as the voice of reason when others wanted to waste hours responding to whatever latest 'outrage' our opponents had committed. He also appears to be biologically incapable of getting indigestion, however fast he eats.

Sara Bashford, my constituency office manager. Sara started working for me before the 2010 election, set up my constituency office after I was elected and has run it for the last six years. If people think I am a good local MP, it is largely down to her. Her only flaws are a reckless disregard for the placement of apostrophes and her habit of agreeing we're going to walk home after a big night out, then hailing a cab after the first ten metres, leaving me to walk home alone.

Mario Creatura, who worked in my Westminster office as well as being one of our most dedicated activists. Cruelly labelled my 'gobby factotum' by our opponents, I like to think of him as the Boy Wonder to my Caped Crusader. An absolutely invaluable member of my team, except when he told the *Croydon Advertiser*, 'Gavin's not the most technically minded person, he generally has no idea.' This is not true. Few people have a better understanding of the Sinclair ZX Spectrum...

Katrina Jones, my Westminster office manager. As efficient as Sara and skilled with apostrophes into the bargain. She hadn't been involved in politics at all before she came to work for me, which meant she brought a different and very valuable perspective to our deliberations. Plus she bakes great cakes. And she's the only person I've ever met who uses half their annual leave to have their hair done. Seriously.

Tim Pollard, then the deputy leader and now the leader of the Conservative group on Croydon Council. He designed all our literature and filmed and produced our videos. This was probably the least pleasant role in the whole campaign since it involved putting up with my constant desire to tinker, which on the whole Tim did without losing his temper (although there was one rather heated conversation after I completely redrafted a video script he had written). He was also my opponent of choice when I wanted to take out my frustrations with the campaign on the tennis court (I let him win for morale purposes, obviously).

Good to go

The strategy I've described in this chapter was agreed at a campaign team meeting on 7 June 2014, just sixteen days after our defeat in the council elections.

I may have been up a well-known creek, but it hadn't taken us long to design a paddle. Now it was time to put it to use.

Chapter 4

Recruitment agency

THE COUNCIL ELECTION campaign had shown that we needed more activists. Labour had brought in people from across south London. Because we weren't a target seat, we weren't able to do that on the same scale and our existing activist base was no match for their imported numbers.

The disparity had been particularly apparent on council election polling day. Labour had far more volunteers out knocking on doors and as a result they managed to get a higher proportion of their supporters to turn out to vote. If we'd had a few more people in Ashburton, we would have got at least eight more votes and hence won at least one extra seat, possibly more. It was that simple: a lack of boots on the ground cost us a seat. And if we didn't do something about it, it might happen again in 2015.

I felt very strongly that there were lots of people out there who would have been prepared to get involved, but there had been two barriers stopping this from happening. First, many of our ward branches were run by people who were either sitting councillors or interested in becoming councillors. It wasn't in their interests to get new people involved because such people might subsequently decide they fancied becoming a councillor too. Second, even where the will to recruit new members was there we weren't very good at converting expressions of interest into active involvement.

The first barrier was easy to get around, at least in the short term. For the next twelve months, all that mattered was finding people who were prepared to help deliver leaflets or, even better, knock on doors. It didn't matter whether those people got involved with their local branch committee or not because the campaign was being centrally run.

The second barrier was tougher. Even when you do everything right some people don't get any further than an initial expression of interest. You knock on their door and, unprompted, they say they are keen to help. You get their email address and promise to send them details of future campaigning sessions, thinking you've struck gold. They reply to your email straight away saying they'll be coming on Saturday.

Then they don't turn up.

So you send them another email and they reply saying something cropped up and promising to come next Saturday.

Again they don't turn up.

You email them again and this time they don't reply so you give up on them.

You can't blame people. Maybe they were just being polite when you first met them and they offered to help. Maybe their partner wasn't keen when they discussed it with them. Maybe something else really did come up.

Other people make it to their first canvassing session. You spend a lot of time talking them through what to do, pair them up with one of your friendliest canvassers and invite them to join the group at the pub afterwards. It all seems to go very well, but they never come again.

Again, you can't blame them. Maybe they expected it to be like an episode of *The West Wing* and, once they learnt the truth, decided that knocking on doors on freezing winter evenings and developing a sixth sense for the blood-hungry Jack Russell lurking behind the letterbox wasn't for them.

The bottom line is you're never going to get all the people who express an interest in helping actively involved. If even half of them end up helping, you're doing well. That means you're going to spend quite a bit of your time on dead ends. Of those where you do succeed, most will happily deliver leaflets, but won't want to knock on doors.

Sometimes, however, you really do strike gold. Jason Cummings, a key member of my campaign team who now runs my Westminster office, got involved in the Conservative Party because Lindsay Frost knocked on his door one night in the run-up to the 2010 election. Amy Pollard, who played a key role in recruiting new activists in the 2015 campaign, got involved because I wrote to residents in her area encouraging people to put their name forward to be local councillors. When you find someone like Jason or Amy, all the hours spent following up dead ends are suddenly worthwhile because, at a constituency level, just a few dedicated people like them can make the world of difference.

There were five things we did to get more people involved. None of them were in any way ground-breaking: it was just a question of consistently getting the basics right.

Keep asking!

Very few people will spontaneously contact a political party to say, 'What I would really like to do with my spare time is deliver thousands of leaflets and knock on hundreds of doors for you.' In fact, I think I'd be suspicious of anyone who contacted us out of the blue in this way. It's not just me who thinks like that either. In Chapter 2 I mentioned that when one of our councillors, Phil Thomas, goes on holiday to the US, he often contacts the local Republican Party office offering to help. I sometimes get emails saying, 'Do you know this guy? Is he for real?' Zealots like Phil aside, if you want people to help you, you have to ask – and keep on asking.

We started the campaign by delivering a letter from Boris Johnson to every household, except those we knew were definitely not Conservative supporters, inviting people to join him at my campaign launch on 22 September. The message was simple:

> If you share my view that Gavin's a great local MP, why don't you come along? Croydon Central is a marginal seat and Ed Miliband and his team will be working hard to get their candidate elected. If Gavin is going to win, he'll need support from people like you. Whether you can deliver a few leaflets, host a meeting with your neighbours in your home, donate a few pounds or display a poster at election time, every little helps.

We included a leaflet setting out my key achievements (see pages 248–9).

In the event, nearly 400 people attended, some of whom had never been involved in politics before.

In February, I sent a letter to everyone canvassed as Conservative, probable Conservative, Conservative/UKIP waverer or Liberal Democrat who preferred us to Labour asking for their help (see pages 260–61). We also trained canvassers to ask anyone who told them they were a strong Conservative supporter if they would help with the campaign.

The house call

Getting someone to offer to help is only the beginning. Next, you have to make sure that each and every offer is followed up.

The most common way in which people will offer to help is to deliver leaflets in their local area. In the three wards with Conservative councillors, one or more of our councillors took responsibility for managing the network of deliverers: Sue Winborn in Fairfield, Andy Stranack and Margaret Mead in Heathfield and Richard Chatterjee in Shirley. This involved contacting people who'd offered to help with delivery to confirm they were willing to do so and agree with them which roads they would do. Then when we had a leaflet to deliver, the co-ordinator counted out the right number of leaflets for each deliverer and took the leaflets round to the deliverers' homes. This was quite a time-consuming exercise – each ward has about 6,000 homes so if you work on the basis of each deliverer dropping to about 200 homes, you're looking at about thirty deliverers per ward.

In the other five wards, there were no Conservative councillors to take on this role. My agent Ian Parker therefore took responsibility for Addiscombe and Woodside, Jason Cummings took Fieldway and New Addington and Cllr Richard Chatterjee kindly volunteered to take Ashburton in addition to his responsibilities in Shirley. By his own admission, Richard isn't the keenest canvasser, but he did an outstanding job rebuilding the delivery network in Ashburton.

Less common, and consequently more valuable, are people who offer to help out with canvassing. We called round on such people to try to get them to commit to joining us on a specific date. We divided these house calls up between me, Mario Creatura and Amy Pollard. Mario and Amy were the perfect people to make such calls: they were young and energetic and presented exactly the right image. As for me, I was neither young nor energetic, but I *was* the candidate, which helped.

A team people want to be part of

The third thing we did was probably the most important, but also the most ephemeral. We tried to create a team people wanted to be part of.

First impressions count. We therefore tried to ensure that at every canvassing session we had a mix of people from different backgrounds, so that if someone new turned up they felt there were other people like them in attendance. The more your team resembles a normal cross-section of society, the more likely new people are to get involved. And the more people you have involved, the more other people want to be part of the team. It's a virtuous circle (or, conversely, a vicious circle if you get this wrong).

As well as ensuring we had a good mix of people, we made sure there was a social side to what we did. On Saturdays, we'd have a pub lunch between the morning and afternoon canvassing sessions at either the Builders Arms in Addiscombe, the Crown in Shirley or the Harvester in Addington Village (thanks to all three for looking after us so well). We also organised regular nights out for the core team.

One of the things that made the campaign bearable was the fantastic team we built. Some of my colleagues find it hard to believe that I actually enjoy canvassing. One of the reasons is that the people I do it with are not just people who've volunteered to help me. They're my friends.

Time well spent

As well as building a team people wanted to be part of, it was important that people felt the time they were giving up was being well used. That meant the organisation of the campaign had to be meticulous. If people volunteered to help with delivery, they should be given a clear map explaining which homes they should deliver to and the right number of leaflets for those homes. If people came canvassing, the sessions should be well organised with a clear briefing at the start, the right amount of work for each team, a map showing which roads needed to be canvassed, canvass cards for those roads, calling cards to leave at homes where nobody was in, clear instructions about where to meet at the end of the session and experienced canvassers on hand to take any new people under their wings.

Ian Parker and Jason Cummings did a great job on this throughout the campaign.

Did I say thank you?

Finally, it was crucial to make sure people knew just how much I valued their help, particularly those who were giving up a large chunk of their spare time. I went to great lengths to do this – not just obvious things like sending thank-you texts after canvass sessions and publicly thanking people in my regular emails to activists, but holding Christmas drinks at our home and inviting people over for dinner.

Didn't we do well?

Slowly but surely we built up our activist team, getting new people involved – some of whom, such as John Broadfoot and Robert Ward, would make a big contribution to the campaign – as well as reactivating people like Emma Hayward and Michael O'Dwyer who'd been involved in the past but had, for various reasons, dropped out. Although we had nothing like the same level of help from outside Croydon as Labour, there were a few people – like Jonny Cope, a former Croydon activist now living in Streatham, and Melanie McLean, a former parliamentary candidate in Islington – who were absolute stars. I even managed to get two of the people who had stood against me in 2010 involved: Michael Castle, who had stood as an independent and was well known in Fieldway ward; and John Cartwright, who had stood as the Monster Raving Loony Party candidate (I believe he was also their shadow Minister for Chocolate, so this was a high-level defection). By the end of the campaign, I had a database of over 500 people who I would email every evening setting out what we were doing the next day and including any urgent requests for help.

Activists from both parties would tweet photos of the teams their party had out that day, which gave us a valuable insight as to whether we were winning the boots-on-the-ground battle. Initially we matched Labour, but as polling day approached and they began to get more and more help from outside Croydon they began to edge ahead.[8] However, the gap was nowhere near as big as it had been in the council election campaign.

The key was that we managed to create a great team spirit. Everyone who came from outside to help commented on it. It was a campaign people wanted to be part of. Looking back now, my abiding memory is of Keith Pearson canvassing in Shirley Oaks village a few days before his 90th birthday. Keith had been treasurer of Croydon Conservatives when I first got involved. He had been retired from campaigning for some time. He couldn't walk very quickly and he was a bit deaf, but here he was back out canvassing again. 'I think this is going to be my last campaign,' he told me, 'but I am ending on a high note.'

And so he was.

8 Their dependence on outside help also had its drawbacks. We had regular reports from electors that they had raised a local issue with a Labour canvasser who, presumably not being from the area, was completely unaware of it and so had nothing to say in response.

Chapter 5

Show me the money

IT WAS ALL very well planning to have a glitzy launch and deliver more literature than Labour, but these things cost money – money that we just didn't have.

A guessing game

We needed to fundraise – and because of the way in which the law that limits how much each campaign can spend works, we needed to do it fast.

There are two separate periods during which spending is controlled. The first covers the period before Parliament is dissolved and the election proper gets underway. We call this 'the long campaign'. It starts four years and seven months from when Parliament first sits after the previous general election (now that we have fixed five-year parliaments, this means just under five months before polling day) and runs until the day before Parliament is dissolved. For the 2015 election, this meant it started on 19 December 2014 and ran until 29 March 2015. The second controlled period covers the last few weeks from the dissolution of Parliament until polling day. We call this 'the short campaign'. The exact limits for each period vary from constituency to constituency depending on the size of the electorate. For Croydon Central, they were £35,288.62 and £13,287.48 respectively.

These limits are there to stop a candidate who is very wealthy or has very wealthy backers from being able to 'buy' an election by massively outspending their opponents. They are set high enough, however, to ensure that candidates who have more support and therefore more people willing to donate to their campaign are able to spend a bit more than those with less support. The two separate controlled periods are there to incentivise candidates to campaign over a period of time, rather than simply splurging £50,000 in the last few weeks.

We believed we could raise more than the £50,000 we were allowed to spend over the two controlled periods. If we wanted to spend every penny that we raised, we therefore needed to start spending before the first controlled period began on 19 December. This left us with a dilemma. We didn't know exactly how much we were going to be able to raise, so we didn't know how much we could spend before the long campaign started and still have enough money left to spend the maximum allowed during both the long and short campaigns.

Imagine we spent £20,000 before the long campaign started, but ended up raising only £50,000 in total. We'd then have just £30,000 left to spend during the long and short campaigns, well below the maximum amount allowed. Just as bad, imagine we spent £20,000 before the start of the long campaign, but ended up raising £100,000. We'd then be left sitting on £30,000 we couldn't actually spend!

We didn't want to be playing a guessing game. We needed to know as quickly as possible how much money we were going to be able to raise in order that we could make rational decisions about how much to spend before the legal limit kicked in.

Setting a target

Some of the things that count towards the spending limits during the two controlled periods – for example, a proportion of the costs of the staff who work for Croydon Conservatives and the costs of running our office – were already budgeted for. We calculated that we needed to raise an additional £32,000 if we were to spend at the legal maximum during both the long and short campaigns.

As well as spending at the legal maximum during the two controlled periods, we wanted to campaign hard in the six months before the legal limit kicked in. We therefore set ourselves a target of raising £60,000.

Who to approach?

I started by asking my local party and the Conservative group on Croydon Council for support. Between them, they provided about £25,000.

Here was clear evidence of the benefits of the way in which the Conservative Party in Croydon is structured. In most parts of the country, there is a separate Conservative Association in every parliamentary constituency, each with its own office if it can afford it. In Croydon, we had merged the three associations to form Croydon Conservative Federation. This had two clear benefits. First, the economies of scale that came from only having one office and sharing staff meant that a higher proportion of the funds that we raised could be spent on campaigning. Second, because my local party included the strongly Conservative areas of Croydon South, it was in a much stronger financial position than if it had just been Croydon Central Conservative Association. Most MPs in marginal seats would not have got such generous support from their local party.

I also benefited from the fact that I had been a councillor in Croydon for twelve years before becoming an MP and had continued to work very closely with the Conservative group since my election. Most MPs in marginal seats would not have got such generous support from their Conservative group either.

We still needed to raise an additional £35,000. The least time-consuming way of doing this would have been to find one extremely generous person who could afford to write a cheque for the whole lot. Even if such a person existed, however, it wouldn't have looked good to have my entire campaign paid for by one person. At the other extreme, I could have tried to get everyone who was thinking of voting Conservative to give me £1.50. Even if this were achievable, it would entail approaching about 20,000 people and we didn't have the time to do that.

We tried to strike a balance between these two extremes by raising a few thousand pounds from small donations (we sent an appeal to everyone who had told us they were a Conservative supporter) and also trying to find twenty or so people each of whom was prepared to give £1,000 or more. Most of the people we approached for these large donations were Croydon residents. However, we also approached a couple of donors to the national Conservative Party, Sir Michael Hintze and Alexander Temerko.[9]

I want to take this opportunity to publicly thank everyone who made a donation to my campaign. My Labour opponent got huge support from Labour HQ. I wasn't getting any help from Conservative HQ, so without the support of these donors there's no way I would have been able to match Labour's campaign.

---

9 Candidates are (rightly) required by law to declare all large donations to the Electoral Commission so that voters can see who is funding their campaigns; if you're interested, you can find the information for my campaign at www.electoralcommission.org.uk.

There is one person I need to single out. His name is Mark Fullbrook. I've worked with Mark on a few occasions down the years. He is close to Sir Michael and Alexander, so I gave him a call and he kindly offered to make the approaches for me. A few days later, he called me back to say he had secured two donations totalling £12,500. Because time was of the essence at this point in the campaign, we signed off a major direct mail project before these donations had reached our account. CCHQ then intervened. They felt that I didn't need all the money Mark had secured because I wasn't a target seat and convinced one of the donors to halve his donation. Mark was so embarrassed he made up the money out of his own pocket, an act of true generosity I won't forget.

The worst job in the world

I hope my passion for campaigning shines through these pages. There are only two things I don't enjoy: counts and fundraising. I've discovered I can get away with not turning up at the count until the result is about to be declared, but these days candidates have no real option but to get involved in fundraising.

There was a time when that wasn't the case. When I started working in the Campaigning Department in the late 1990s, some of the older agents still referred to candidates as 'a legal necessity'. The agent would raise the cash, write the leaflets and organise the campaign – the candidate just provided the name to go on the ballot paper.

Those days have gone. Today, if people are going to give money to a political campaign, they want – not unreasonably – to get to know the candidate they are supporting. I'm very happy to go and talk politics with anyone, but I hated asking for a donation at the end of the conversation. There were, however, bills to be paid, so how I felt about it really wasn't important.

No strings attached

I only have one rule when it comes to fundraising: never, ever accept a donation with strings attached. If someone wants to give you some of their hard-earned money because they believe you are the best person to represent that constituency in Parliament, that's fantastic. If they're giving you money in return for something, however, it's toxic. It means you are no longer free to do what's right for your constituents; you're beholden to someone. Even if you were going to do what the donor wants anyway, it's still a bad idea because it can be used against you.

My Labour opponent, Sarah Jones, made this mistake in accepting a £10,000 donation from Lord Oakeshott, a Liberal Democrat peer who was not a fan of the coalition. A strong supporter of our membership of the EU, he wanted to stop the people of this country being given their say on this issue in a referendum. So he gave a total of £600,000 to thirty Labour candidates in marginal seats, fifteen Liberal Democrat MPs and candidates in marginal seats and the Green MP Caroline Lucas, all of whom shared his opposition to a referendum.

This was a gift to me. I was trying to convince Conservatives who were tempted to vote UKIP that if they did so they would get a Labour MP, Ed Miliband as Prime Minister and no referendum. All of a sudden, a rich man with no connection to Croydon announces that he has given my opponent £10,000 because she has promised to vote against having a referendum.

Success beyond our wildest dreams

I might not have enjoyed asking, but time after time I was getting the answer I was hoping for. In the end, we raised nearly £90,000, 50 per cent more than our target, and we raised most of this before the start of the long campaign. This meant we could spend a huge amount before the legal controls began, confident that we would still be able to spend as much as we were allowed during the two controlled periods *and* have a reserve in case the national result was very tight and we were faced with another election a few months later.

If we didn't win on 7 May, it wouldn't be for a lack of money.

Chapter 6

On the knocker

EVER WONDERED WHY political activists spend hours of their lives walking from house to house like Jehovah's Witnesses with coloured rosettes?

Canvassing may look like door-to-door selling, but in fact it's opinion research. We don't knock on people's doors to persuade them to vote Conservative. We do it to get accurate information about how people are likely to vote and the issues they are concerned about.

Some people like to keep how they vote private. They're perfectly entitled to do so. It can, however, be to your advantage to tell canvassers how you're planning to vote. For starters, if you tell a canvasser for one candidate that you are definitely voting for their candidate or indeed for a different candidate, they are unlikely to call back – they've found out what they need to know. And if you mention that you are concerned about a particular issue, that information should get passed back to the candidate and they may get in touch with you about it. It's actually a good opportunity to make your views known – and you haven't even had to leave your house.

What do we want this information for?

Canvassing is an essential element of any political campaign. We want to know how people are thinking of voting and the issues they are concerned about in order to inform how and about what we communicate with them.

To do this, we first store all the information on a database, placing people into one of a number of voter types, each of which has a one-letter code. The main ones are:

C	Conservative
P	Probable Conservative
S	Labour (S stands for socialist – this code was created a long time ago, but with the election of Jeremy Corbyn as leader of the Labour Party it's now appropriate again)
T	Normally Labour, but possibly Conservative this time
L	Liberal Democrat
M	Normally Liberal Democrat, but possibly Conservative this time
N	Nationalist
Z	Normally Nationalist, but possibly Conservative this time
K	UKIP
G	Green
B	BNP
A	Against (we didn't get time to find out who the elector is voting for, but the violence with which the door was slammed suggests it is not us)
W	Won't vote
X	Won't say
U	Undecided

We then use this information to target our efforts.

An obvious example is polling day. We call on those people who have told us that they are thinking of voting for us to remind them it's polling day and encourage them to go and support us.[10] We don't want to remind those who told us they wouldn't vote for us in a month of Sundays. If we didn't have information about which people are thinking of voting for us and which people have no intention of doing so, we would be reduced to knocking on every door, thereby spending much of our time reminding our opponents' supporters to go out and vote against us.

Another example is direct mail. We target this at people who have told us they are undecided, but might vote for us – there's no point wasting resources on people who have already made up their mind. And we write to them about the issues they've told us they care most about. For example, we might send a mailing to floating voters who've told us that they are concerned about the NHS, which sets out how the Conservative Party will provide the extra £8 billion NHS senior management say it needs and points out that Labour have refused to match this commitment.

Sometimes, we supplement the data we get from canvassing with the record of who voted at each election. This is information we can buy from the local council[11] and it helps us further refine our targeting. For example, we might send postal vote application forms to people who've told us they are Conservative supporters, but who didn't vote at the last election.

We can also supplement our canvassing data with demographic and consumer data we can buy from the private sector. A good example is MOSAIC, a classification system developed by a company called Experian that divides people into sixty-six pithily titled types (for example, 'Bank of Mum and Dad' for 'well-off families

---

10 If it's a general election, everyone will know it's polling day from all the media coverage, but you'd be surprised how many people can be blissfully unaware that it's polling day for council elections.

11 People are often surprised that political parties can acquire this data given elections are meant to be secret ballots. However, the law says that while *how* you voted is secret, *whether* you voted is not.

in upmarket suburban homes where parents are still supporting their grown-up children'). We can cross-match our canvassing and polling data with MOSAIC to build a predictive model showing how likely people in different MOSAIC types are to be Conservative supporters or key target voters. We can then use this to decide where we should focus our canvassing (there's not much point canvassing in an area where we are likely to find very few Conservative supporters or waverers) or, in areas where we haven't done enough canvassing, as a substitute for canvassing data (it's only a predictive model so it won't be 100 per cent accurate, but it's better than nothing).

How do we know who lives at each property?

We have a good idea of who lives at each address because all candidates are entitled to a copy of the electoral register – a record of the people at each property who are entitled to vote in elections. This information can be up to a year out-of-date, however, so we won't know if someone has recently moved or died. The latter situation is one every canvasser dreads. You knock on a door and an old lady answers. You ask about her concerns and how she is thinking of voting, then ask about her husband. Her eyes well up and she tells you that he recently passed away. All you can do is apologise profusely, offer your sincere condolences and promise to correct your database so that it doesn't happen again, but you feel terrible about it.

Can't we get the information we need by telephoning people, rather than knocking on their doors?

Yes. Telephone canvassing is actually the quickest way to get the information we need, but most people are ex-directory so we can't reach them. It's also probably less accurate than door-to-door canvassing as there are no clues from body language for the canvasser to pick up on.

We also distribute survey forms for people to complete themselves (we either post people the forms with a reply-paid return envelope or knock on people's doors, give them a form and say we'll call back in an hour or so to pick it up). When someone from a political party asks an elector how they're going to vote, there's a risk the elector will say what they think the canvasser wants to hear – either out of politeness or because they want to get them off their doorstep or phone. Getting people to complete a form in private is therefore probably the most accurate method of acquiring voting intention data. The problem, though, is that response rates are typically only around 10 per cent. That's why door-to-door canvassing is the main method – we can reach everyone apart from people who live in gated developments and, unless someone lets us in, blocks of flats where access is intercom-controlled.

The drawback is that it is incredibly time consuming. In a two-hour session, I might knock on fifty to sixty doors. There will be no one in at half these properties and a few people will say they're just eating or putting the kids to bed so they don't want to talk. I will probably end up acquiring data for about twenty-five properties. What's more, there may be more than one voter at each property and I am unlikely to get information for all of them – people often don't know how other members of their household vote, and some members of the household may be out or may not want to come to the door.

The accuracy problem

As well as being labour-intensive (or Conservative-intensive, in our case), you have to be careful that the information you get from canvassing is reliable. The reason this is difficult is that most people are just too damn nice.

Once you introduce yourself as being from a particular political party, most strong supporters of other parties will be too polite to tell you they'll only be ready to vote for you when Hell gets its first skating rink. Instead they'll say that they haven't made their minds up yet or they're waiting to read the manifestos or they vote for the individual not the party so they need to read up on the candidates. Then there are those, as mentioned above, who are so desperate to get you off their doorstep or phone that they'll tell you what they think you want to hear. Of course, there are a few people who take great pleasure in telling you in no uncertain terms how much they hate you. What they don't know is that in doing so they are giving you exactly what you want – an unambiguous voting intention.

These problems are exacerbated by the fact that canvassing is carried out by volunteers, many of whom have never been trained. As a result, some think their job is to find as many Conservatives as possible or, even worse, to persuade people to vote Conservative, rather than to acquire accurate information. They'll come away from a door saying, 'They were Labour, but I've talked them round.' How likely is that? Is someone really going to change their voting intention as a result of a two-minute conversation with a stranger on their doorstep?

Because these enthusiastic but misguided canvassers are trying to get what they think is the 'right' answer, they ask leading questions such as, 'Gavin's a really hard-working MP. Can he count on your support?' This makes it even more likely that the elector will tell them what they want to hear. It's vital to give people 'permission' to tell you they don't vote for you by asking the question in a neutral way: 'Are you thinking of voting Labour, UKIP, Conservative or not voting at all?' I never put the Conservative Party first in the list and I always include the 'not voting' option. Just under a third of the electorate in Croydon Central didn't vote on 7 May 2015, but relatively few of the tens of thousands of people we canvassed were recorded as 'Won't vote'. Many people are too embarrassed to admit they don't vote unless you make it easy for them to do so. I obviously wish they did vote, but when I'm canvassing I'm not trying to change their mind; I'm trying to get accurate information about what they are likely to do.

There are lots of other mistakes canvassers make if they are not well trained. Here are a few of my personal favourites:

1. *Not checking the name of the person who answers the door.* Our intrepid canvasser knocks at 1 Station Road. According to the electoral register, two people who are eligible to vote live here, Mr and Mrs Smith. The canvasser speaks to a woman, who tells him she is a Conservative supporter, so the canvasser records Mrs Smith as a C. In fact, the Smiths have moved and the person he spoke to was the new tenant. When she comes onto the register, the information the canvasser obtained, which was recorded against Mrs Smith, will be lost.

2. *Assuming that everyone in the house votes the same way.* When I'm training people how to canvass, I often tell the story of an elderly couple whose door I knocked on in Shirley Oaks Village. The husband came to the door, told me that Doomsday would come before anyone in the house voted Conservative and slammed the door in my face. A few minutes later, his wife tiptoed down the road to tell me she was a Conservative. They'd been married for over fifty years, but she'd never told him how she voted.

3. *Not asking follow-up questions.* Our canvasser has now moved on to 3 Station Road. This time he remembers to check whether the person who opens the door is indeed the Mr Ahmed who is on the electoral register. It is and he says he hasn't made up his mind yet, so our canvasser records him as 'Undecided'. However, if he'd asked Mr Ahmed whether he was considering voting

> Conservative, he'd have laughed and told you his parents would turn in their grave if he did that. He's actually undecided between Labour and the Greens and should have been recorded as 'Against'. Because our canvasser didn't ask a follow-up question, we're going to waste time and money calling back on him and sending him targeted literature.

Some of our canvassing for the council elections certainly hadn't been accurate – it had suggested we were going to win Ashburton and Waddon. And this time we were trying to do something much more ambitious, identifying very specific groups of floating voters – disillusioned Conservatives who were tempted by UKIP, Liberal Democrat supporters who preferred us to Labour and undecided voters who preferred David Cameron to Ed Miliband or wanted to keep me as their local MP. If we were to have any chance of doing this, we needed to change how we canvassed.

Inventing our own solution

In the Conservative Party's target seats, CCHQ were using a new canvassing script with electors being asked to rank the likelihood of them voting for each party on a scale of 1 to 10 as well as who they preferred as Prime Minister and what kind of government they wanted after the election.

In principle, this was a much better way of doing things. It would give far more detailed and therefore useful information about floating voters than a 'Probable' or 'Undecided' code, differentiating between those who were undecided between Conservative and UKIP, those who were undecided between Conservative and Labour, those who were undecided between Conservative and Liberal Democrat and those who were not going to vote Conservative but were undecided about who they would vote for. The downside, however, was that each conversation would take a long time and my instinct was that many electors would refuse to answer that many questions.

One of the few advantages of not being a target seat was that we didn't have to follow the CCHQ script – we were free to do things our own way. Like CCHQ, we wanted to avoid having lots of people recorded simply as 'Undecided'. This didn't really tell us anything useful. Were such electors considering voting Conservative or were they undecided between other parties? If the former, what was the lever we could use to move them into our column? We also wanted to differentiate Conservatives who were tempted by UKIP from people who were definitely going to vote for Farage's party. And we wanted to find a simpler, less time-consuming way of doing both these things than the new CCHQ script.

We were limited by the fact that we couldn't invent any new codes (it's a national system so only CCHQ can do this). We could, though, abuse one or more of the existing codes. In the end we came up with four changes:

1. We abused the Z code, which was meant to be for people who were normally SNP or Plaid Cymru supporters, but were thinking of voting Conservative this time. Scottish and Welsh nationalists are thin on the ground in Croydon so this was effectively a spare code for us. We therefore used Z for Conservatives who admitted to being tempted by UKIP and UKIP supporters we judged we had a chance of getting back. The K code – the official code for UKIP supporters – we would reserve for those who were definitely going to vote UKIP. If CCHQ looked closely at our data, they might wonder why Croydon had suddenly become a hotbed of support for Scottish and/or Welsh independence, but we'd cross that bridge if we came to it.

2. We asked Liberal Democrats whether they preferred us to Labour. If they did, we would code them as M (normally Liberal

Democrat, but considering voting Conservative this time); if they didn't, we would code them as Liberal Democrats.

3. We asked all the undecideds whether they preferred David Cameron or Ed Miliband as Prime Minister. If they preferred Cameron, we would give them a 'David Cameron for Prime Minister' flag.

4. We asked the undecideds who had no preference between David Cameron and Ed Miliband what they thought about me. If they had a strongly positive view, we would give them a 'Gavin Barwell for MP' flag.

These changes, if implemented by all our canvassers, would allow us to identify our four target voter groups.

We're not just interested in how you vote (honest!)

The primary purpose of canvassing is to gather information on electors' voting intentions, but there's lots of other useful data we tried to collect while we were at it.

Information on an issue an elector was concerned about was very useful. This might be a piece of casework I could take up or it might be a national issue I could write to the elector about.

We also tried to collect electors' email addresses. I sent out a regular email bulletin, keeping people informed of what I was doing. People who received this bulletin generally had a much more favourable view of me. The more email addresses we could get, the better I would do.

Finally, when we found strong Conservatives we asked them if they were prepared to help with the campaign. We needed all the help we could get.

Training the team

If we wanted our canvassers to implement a strategy this complex, they were going to need training.

We had a long discussion about whether to produce a script. My view was that the key to being an effective canvasser was to put people at their ease and that meant being yourself, not trying to slavishly follow some pre-ordained wording. What was important was that the questions were asked in a certain order and that the canvasser gave the elector all the options, rather than asking a leading question. The exact language didn't matter. So instead of a script, we produced a flowchart (see page 247).

When we door-to-door canvass, we do so in teams to make it more sociable. When you work in a team, one person has a clipboard with the canvass cards showing which electors live at which properties (we call this 'doing the board'). They don't knock on any doors themselves; instead, they send the other members of the team to specific properties, telling them who is on the register at those properties, and, when they return, record what they report on the canvass cards.

If we wanted to get people to adopt our new approach, the people doing the boards would be key. They needed to check that canvassers were doing it right: whether people who said they were Conservatives were being asked whether they were tempted by UKIP; whether people who said they were undecided were being asked who they preferred as Prime Minister and what they thought of me; whether strong Conservatives were being asked if they would help with the campaign; and whether everyone was being asked for their email address.

In the past, we'd often put the weakest canvasser in charge of the board. Given their key role in enforcing the new approach, we started using some of our best people in this role. It's not a job for the faint of heart. I remember running a board during the Crewe

& Nantwich by-election. My team of canvassers consisted of one George Osborne, then the shadow Chancellor, and some of his advisers. His team were shocked when I made him go back to a family he had just canvassed as Conservatives because he hadn't checked whether they would take a poster. Greatly to his credit, he didn't pull rank: he went back and we ended up with another poster site.

We organised a briefing before our first canvass session on 28 June 2014. Would people who had been canvassing for years turn up? Or would they feel as if they were grandmothers invited to an egg-sucking seminar?

I was over the moon with the turnout. Virtually all our senior activists were there. Most people clearly recognised that something had gone wrong with our canvassing for the council elections and wanted to have a discussion about what we could to put it right.

After the first canvassing session, we reviewed the cards. Most people were using the new codes and flags, but not everyone. As a result, I repeated a short version of the briefing at the start of every canvass session until everyone was well and truly sick of it. It worked, though. By the end of the campaign we had identified significant numbers of each of our target groups. We were then able to send these crucial swing voters targeted direct mail and call on them in the final days of the campaign. The painstaking work of acquiring accurate information about electors' voting intentions ultimately proved crucial to our victory.

Chapter 7

Barwell online

THE 2015 ELECTION was the first digital election in British political history. The parties had experimented with online campaigning in 2010, but this time it was a fully integrated part of our campaigns both nationally and locally.

Its potential is obvious. We used to rely on four main channels to communicate our message: broadcast media, which is required to be politically balanced; print media, which has been hit by falling newspaper circulation; paid media – mostly adverts in newspapers and on billboards (we are not allowed to advertise on TV or radio) – which is expensive; and direct marketing, either by posting material to target voters, which is expensive, or hand-delivering it, which is slow and requires an army of volunteers. With the advances in the digital world, we now have a number of means of communicating with people that are quick and very cheap.

That said, this election marked a transition from the old style of campaigning to the new, not a whole new world. We were able to reach a large proportion of the electorate online but by no means everyone, so we had to continue with traditional forms of campaigning alongside the new technologies.

You've got email

The first form of online campaigning I adopted was mass emails. I started building a database of email addresses and sending out regular email bulletins as soon as I was selected as a candidate back in 2008. When constituents contacted me with a piece of casework or to let me know their view on something we were debating in Parliament, I always asked if I could add their email address to my database when I replied. When we asked people to sign a petition or complete a survey form, we always asked for their email address. We also started asking for them when we were canvassing. I was initially sceptical about this, but it turned out that most people are much happier to let you have their email address than their telephone number.

At the start of the campaign, I had about 7,000 email addresses. Over the next eleven months, we managed to increase that to about 10,000. This allowed me to communicate with about a quarter of my electorate (perhaps more – we picked up evidence that some people were forwarding these emails on) without having to pay to print a leaflet.

More importantly, it removed the inevitable time lag you get with leaflets, which need to be written, printed and then delivered through 50,000 letterboxes. It is difficult to overstate just how important this was. If a major story broke, it meant I could communicate my message to a significant proportion of my electorate very quickly.

As the sitting MP, I had a clear advantage over my Labour

opponent. First, I'd had seven years to build up a database; she was only selected just over a year and a half before polling day. And whereas she had to rely solely on campaigning to collect email addresses, lots of my constituents emailed me as their MP and then gave me permission to store their email address and send them email bulletins. I had to be careful, however. While it's extremely easy to send someone an email, it's equally easy for them to unsubscribe from any more messages. I was keen to communicate regularly with my constituents, but I didn't want to overdo it. I tried to send out email bulletins only when I had something significant to say – on average, probably once every two or three weeks.

I could tell from the responses I received and the number of people who unsubscribed which ones were a hit and which ones irritated people. The lesson was clear: the emails needed to be personal, setting out my views instead of just repeating the party line. They also needed to be timely – about something that people might have just seen on the news or a current local issue.

A good example is an email I sent out on the day the news broke about Sir Malcolm Rifkind and Jack Straw being caught offering their services to an undercover reporter for £5,000 a day:

> I love my job. Having the chance to represent my home town in Parliament is a huge honour. But there are times when I really do despair. Today is such a day.
>
> Over the last four and a half years I have done this job to the best of my ability. I was very conscious when I got elected of the understandably low regard in which politicians were held and I've tried to do what I can to restore people's faith. I publish all my expenses claims and the supporting receipts so people can be confident that I'm not on the make. I don't employ family members. I publish my diary so my constituents can see how I spend my time. And I don't have a second job.

Most of the MPs I've met are decent, hard-working people. But every time there's a story like this morning's news about Sir Malcolm Rifkind and Jack Straw, two former Foreign Secretaries, hawking their services for £5,000 a day, all that work is undone.

Sir Malcolm told the undercover reporters, 'You'd be surprised how much free time I have.' As someone who struggles to find enough hours in the day to do the job and be a good husband and father, yes I would.

He goes on, 'Nobody pays me a salary,' which will come as a surprise to taxpayers who are paying him over £80,000 a year.

He then compounded his errors by giving a radio interview in which he implied he couldn't be expected to live on his parliamentary salary – far more than most of my constituents earn.

Jack Straw boasted to the undercover reporters how he 'operated under the radar' and complained how it was 'slightly boring' having to be transparent about his outside earnings.

Mr Straw has suspended himself from the Parliamentary Labour Party and David Cameron has withdrawn the whip from Sir Malcolm, but their remarks will no doubt revive the debate about whether MPs should be allowed second jobs.

As noted above, I find being an MP a full-time job. But there are other MPs who were lawyers or doctors or ran a family business before they got elected and don't want to give up their old job entirely. There is an argument that Parliament benefits from this outside experience. So my view is that MPs should have to be transparent about how much they are earning from other work and who is paying them. Their constituents can then decide at election time whether they are happy with this or not.

But my purpose in writing is to let you know that many MPs feel just as angry about this latest scandal as you do.

Making these emails as personal as possible allowed thousands of people who had never met me, or had only spoken to me briefly, to feel that they knew me. We were aware from our surveys that people who received these email bulletins had a far more favourable view of me. They were one of the most effective things I did in my time as an MP. If you're interested, you can find all my email bulletins at www.gavinbarwell.com/emailbulletinarchive.

Facebook: mass-market social media

As well as email, I started to make use of social media to communicate my message.

Facebook was far and away the best of the social media for communicating with my constituents. First, it is the most widely used. On 24 August 2015, Facebook was accessed by over 1 billion people around the world for the first time (although admittedly not all of them were looking at my page). Second, we could pay to get our message to Facebook users living in particular areas. It wasn't very expensive and we got a great response.

We also put a lot of effort into producing video content for my YouTube channel. At one end of the scale, some of them were professionally produced – the video we showed at the campaign launch and 'The difference a good MP makes' video that we distributed the day before polling day. Others were just filmed on a smartphone when we picked up a local issue while canvassing. If you're interested, you can find them all at www.gavinbarwell.com/videos.

To tweet or not to tweet

The social media channel I am most ambivalent about is Twitter.

For those who are not familiar with it, Twitter allows you to post messages called 'tweets' of no more than 140 characters (you can get around the character limit by including a website link to an article you've written). These messages can be viewed by anyone who goes to your page on the Twitter website, but they are most likely to be seen by other Twitter users who have opted to 'follow' you. If they're interested in something you've tweeted, they can forward or 'retweet' it to their own followers.

To give you an idea, here are three tweets from autumn 2015, available at www.twitter.com/gavinbarwellmp:

> In 3 days time I will be doing my annual 18mile charity walk. This year supporting @secancerhelp More details here http://www.gavin-barwell.com/blog.asp?BlogID=1083

> RT: @bbclaurak Mentioning equality and getting a standing ovation on platform would have been unimaginable at a Tory conference a decade ago [This is a retweet of a tweet by the BBC's political editor Laura Kuenssberg about David Cameron's party conference speech.]

> @Nigel_Farage says UKIP conference celebrating fact we're having EU referendum We wouldn't be if UKIP had got more votes in seats like mine

Over the four and a half years I've been using Twitter, I've sent more than 12,000 messages and at the time of the election I had just short of 10,000 people following me. Most of the people who follow me are fellow politicians, journalists and other political obsessives so it is mainly a tool for communicating with opinion formers. On the other hand, I do also have a reasonable number of constituents among my followers.

Twitter has a number of drawbacks. First, it's high risk. If you say something stupid, as I have on a couple of occasions, it quickly goes viral. Deleting the stupid tweet is no good – in fact, that just makes it worse – because by then someone will already have a screen grab of it. Second, you will get a lot of abuse (most of it from people who lack the courage to reveal who they are) so you need to have a thick skin. Third, it can be quite addictive – if you're not careful, you'll end up spending far too much time on it relative to the electoral return you will get. And fourth, people like me who enjoy a good debate need to be careful not to get involved in tit-for-tat, point-scoring arguments with political opponents that are off-putting to most people.

These drawbacks aside, Twitter can be an incredibly powerful tool for communicating your message to people who might not otherwise see it. There's a story I like to tell to illustrate this.

I was out leafleting in Woodside ward. It was a miserable day, cold and wet, so I was dressed in a hoodie and jeans and had my headphones in. As I walked back up someone's front garden path, I became aware that there was a black couple of about my age waiting to speak to me. My cover had been blown. I apologised for my appearance and asked what I could do for them. The woman said she just wanted to tell me she had enjoyed my recent article on ConservativeHome about how the Conservative Party needed to do more to win support from people from black and minority ethnic communities. I thanked her and then, as politely as I could, suggested that she didn't strike me as the stereotypical ConservativeHome reader. She laughed and said she had never read ConservativeHome before in her life, but she followed me on Twitter and I had tweeted a link to the article.

I suspect this couple wouldn't have read a Conservative-branded leaflet that was put through their letterbox. Social media had allowed me to communicate my personal brand of Conservatism to them. In return for an opportunity to do that, I am prepared to put up with all the abuse Twitter has to offer.

Chapter 8

Tour guide

ONE OF THE perks of my job is that I get to work in one of the most beautiful buildings in the country. It's not just the architecture either – the place is steeped in history. As its proper name – the Palace of Westminster – implies, the Houses of Parliament started out as a royal palace. The first parliaments sat there in the thirteenth century and it became the permanent home of Parliament after 1512 when Henry VIII decided to move out after his apartments were destroyed in a fire. It has been the setting for key events in our history from the trial of Charles I at the end of the Civil War to the vote of no confidence in Chamberlain's government in May 1940 that led to Churchill becoming Prime Minister.

Once I became the MP for Croydon Central, constituents would occasionally contact me asking if I could book them on one of the tours organised by the staff of the Houses of Parliament. I would duly oblige and didn't think too much of it until one day a few years later the MP for Watford, Richard Harrington, told me that he had started showing groups of his constituents around himself and they really appreciated it. I thought that was something I would enjoy doing, so I included an advert in my next email bulletin asking anyone who was interested in a tour to get in touch. I was immediately deluged with requests.

The best times for people to visit are when neither the House of Commons nor the House of Lords are sitting because then you can actually walk onto the floor of both chambers. That means either when Parliament is in recess (roughly speaking when schools are on holiday) or on a Monday morning, a Thursday evening, a Friday afternoon or at the weekend.[12] I therefore set about arranging tours at these times.

Before I conducted my first tour, I went on one of the official ones to see what the guides said. I then adapted their script, leaving out the bits that I didn't think were particularly interesting and adding a few personal stories about my own time as an MP.

My tour starts in Westminster Hall, the only surviving bit of the old Palace of Westminster other than the Jewel Tower, which is now the other side of the road (the rest of the old building burnt down in a fire in 1834). Over the years, Westminster Hall has been home to the most important courts in the country (the trial of King Charles I took place here); members of the royal family have lain in state here following their deaths, as did Churchill and Gladstone, so that people could pay their respects; and, more recently, visiting dignitaries have addressed both Houses of Parliament here. In my time, three people have been given this honour:

---

12 The House of Commons doesn't sit until 2.30 p.m. on Mondays to allow MPs whose constituencies are a long way from London to travel to Westminster on Monday morning rather than Sunday night. It adjourns at 5 p.m. on Thursdays to allow the same MPs to travel home on Thursday evening rather than Friday morning. It doesn't generally sit on Fridays and when it does it adjourns at 2.30 p.m. The House of Lords has broadly similar hours.

the Burmese opposition leader Aung San Suu Kyi, President Barack Obama and Pope Benedict XVI.

Next stop is the beautiful Chapel of St Mary Undercroft, underneath Westminster Hall. The suffragette Emily Davison spent the night of the 1911 census in a broom cupboard just behind the chapel – unable to stand for Parliament or vote in a general election, she wished to make a point by being recorded at the Houses of Parliament in the census records. Then it's on to St Stephen's Hall, the only part of the new palace that was rebuilt exactly as it was before the fire. In the old palace, this room was home to the House of Commons for many years.

Up the steps from St Stephen's is Central Lobby. If neither House is sitting and it's not too busy, you get a great view from here. To the south, you can see the Queen's throne at the end of the House of Lords; to the north, the Speaker's Chair at the end of the House of Commons. Most visitors recognise Central Lobby from the news – it is from here that TV journalists report on what is going on in Parliament.

From there, we make our way down to the Peers' Lobby and through the Aye division lobby, where there is an exact replica of one of the four surviving copies of Magna Carta (in 2015, the 800th anniversary of its signing, all four surviving copies were brought together in Parliament for a special exhibition). Then we go into the Prince's Chamber, which is dedicated to the Tudor period of British history.

Beyond the Prince's Chamber is the Royal Gallery, dominated by two huge paintings: the death of Nelson at the Battle of Trafalgar and the meeting of Wellington and Blücher at the Battle of Waterloo. At the end of the building is the Queen's Robing Room, whose paintings and engravings are dedicated to the legend of King Arthur and the Knights of the Round Table.

We then make our way back into the chamber of the House of Lords, beside which the Commons looks very plain. The key difference between the two chambers is the existence of cross-benches in the House of Lords for those who don't support any political party. You can be an independent in the Commons, but you have to choose to either support or oppose the government – there's no sitting in the middle (except for the Speaker).

Then we follow the long corridor that Black Rod walks down during the annual State Opening of Parliament to the Members' Lobby just outside the House of Commons. Here I talk about my work as a government whip (the whips' offices are just off Members' Lobby). From there we go into the No division lobby, where I describe how we vote by walking through either the Aye or the No lobby. This process is time consuming (each vote takes about fifteen minutes), but the idea is we should be seen to be voting a certain way rather than quickly pressing a button on a keypad. It's in the No lobby that I point out the gifts from countries throughout the Commonwealth that allowed the Commons to be rebuilt after it was destroyed by a bomb during the Second World War – one of the most popular moments of the tour because many of my constituents or their parents or grandparents come from one of those countries.

We end the tour in the chamber of the House of Commons itself. In every group I have taken round, there is always someone who remarks that they're surprised how small it looks. And they're right: it can't seat anywhere near all 650 MPs. When it was rebuilt after being destroyed in the Second World War, Churchill rejected the idea that it should be enlarged so that every MP had their own seat, arguing that 'there should be on great occasions a sense of crowd and urgency'.

The tour normally takes about an hour and a half, a little longer if it's a large group. Afterwards I spend thirty to forty-five minutes answering questions. This is my chance to communicate my passion for my job. I want people to feel able to ask whatever is on their mind, so first I make it clear that they can ask about anything

– what they've seen on the tour, what it's like to be an MP, my background, a local issue or national politics. And then I do my best to give honest, direct answers rather than behaving like a stereotypical politician by avoiding the questions or resorting to spin.

In the run-up to the election, I found some of the question-and-answer sessions quite emotional. People would say, 'I've really enjoyed the tour. Could I come back with my next-door neighbours?' I would reply, 'Yes, but I'm not taking bookings at the moment because I don't know if I'll still be an MP after 7 May.' This really surprised most people. As I mentioned previously, quite a few people weren't aware that they live in a marginal area.

Someone would then ask what I was going to do if I didn't win. I told the truth: I didn't have a clue. The room would go quiet. Afterwards, people would come up to me and wish me luck whatever the result of the election. I was under a huge amount of pressure and this concern for my welfare from people of all political affiliations – so at odds with the crowing about my imminent demise from opponents on Twitter – touched me deeply.

I find doing these tours hugely rewarding on two levels. First, I love showing constituents round Parliament. I feel very strongly that it is *their* Parliament, not a private club for MPs. Second, the question-and-answer sessions are often very useful in getting feedback about national and local issues.

Unexpectedly, the tours also turned out to have a political benefit. In fact, they probably did more to shift people's voting intentions than anything else I did. It became a running joke between Jason Cummings and me. If we were out canvassing and we found someone who had switched sides and was now supporting us, he would get the canvasser to check if they had been on a tour. More than half the time, they had.

So why were they so effective? They weren't in any way political. I went out of my way *not* to use the question-and-answer sessions to score political points because I was conscious that people had come for a tour of Parliament, not a party-political broadcast. In hindsight, I believe they made a difference because anyone who came on a tour got to spend up to two and a half hours with me – enough to get a fair idea of what I'm like as a person. To those people, I was no longer 'the Conservative Party candidate': they knew the person behind the name on the ballot paper and that was often enough to change their voting intention.

My Labour opponents thought it was very funny. They joked that I could get a full-time job showing people round when I lost my seat on 7 May. Little did they know that my time as a tour guide was inadvertently helping me to keep my job.

Chapter 9

Rapid rebuttal

IN ANY CAMPAIGN, it's important to establish psychological dominance over your opponent – to win the intellectual battle so they know that if they use a dodgy statistic or make a claim that isn't true, they'll be caught out.

At a national level, this intellectual battle is largely conducted in the House of Commons and judged by the media. Journalists like Fraser Nelson or those behind Channel 4's FactCheck like nothing more than researching politicians' claims to see if they stand up. At a local level, people can get away with a lot more because there's nothing like the same level of scrutiny. The House of Commons meets most weekdays; Croydon Council meets half a dozen times a year. There's widespread coverage of national politics on broadcast media and in national newspapers; Croydon politics will only be covered in the London media if it's a big story and, aside from community-run TV and radio stations broadcast via the internet, there's no local media apart from the *Croydon Advertiser* and the *Croydon Guardian*, which are only published once a week and aren't distributed throughout the borough. The intellectual battle between the parties is therefore largely unmediated and conducted via Twitter.

I got into politics through debating, which is basically arguing with rules and a time limit. My idea of a good night out is some beers with my best friends and a good discussion about something. We've known each other since we were eleven years old so by now we've argued about pretty much everything it's possible to argue about, most things multiple times (like good wine, a good argument can improve with age).

So if one of the things I needed to do as part of my job was to have the occasional debate on Twitter, well, that wasn't work – it was fun. I think it was my former boss Danny Finkelstein who said in one of his *Times* columns that trying to win an argument on Twitter is like trying to empty the Atlantic Ocean with a teacup. I wielded my teacup with relish.

There was a risk here, however. If I was not careful, I could win the arguments, but harm my chances by doing so. Most people don't like arguing – it makes them feel uncomfortable. And they particularly don't like politicians squabbling like children. One of my best friends, Pete, did me a real favour when he said to me one night that he really didn't like the Gavin Barwell he followed on Twitter (I think the phrase he used was 'argumentative twat'). From then on, I tried to rein in my natural instinct to get into prolonged and acrimonious exchanges with political opponents on Twitter.

I blocked opposition activists who were clearly just trying to goad me and focused solely on Sarah Jones, Steve Reed and senior Labour councillors. And when one of them used a dodgy statistic or made a false claim, I tried to limit myself to one tweet pointing out the facts. I think Pete would say that there has been progress in the right direction, but there's still room for improvement.

I spent a lot of time rebutting false claims. You see something an opponent has said and think, 'That doesn't sound right', but then you have to go away, find out the facts and construct a response. There were countless instances during the campaign, but below are two examples which show how some politicians spin statistics – and how you go about catching them out. There are other examples dotted through the book.

In work, but on benefits

In August 2014, Steve Reed claimed that the number of people in Croydon who were in work but earning so little that they were still entitled to claim housing benefit had increased by 1,100 per cent under the coalition government. This increase was so large that it immediately seemed suspicious. Fortunately, I had felt the same about a very similar claim made the week before by Emma Reynolds, then Labour's housing spokesperson (though her claim related to my constituency, not Croydon as a whole, and to the period since February 2011 rather than since May 2010). I had asked the amazing House of Commons Library for the facts. This was their response:

> Dear Mr Barwell,
>
> We spoke earlier. Please find attached the available data on Housing Benefit (HB) claimants in employment in Croydon. The number of HB claimants in employment and resident in the Croydon Central constituency has risen by 50 per cent between February 2011 and February 2014 (from 2,810 to 4,203). 33 per cent of HB claimants in your constituency are recorded as being in employment as of February 2014 (compared with 31 per cent in London as a whole and 21 per cent nationally). I hope this helps – let us know if you need anything further.

Helpfully, they included a table showing the figures for every parliamentary constituency so I could calculate the equivalent figures for Croydon as a whole. They were 8,552 claimants in February 2011 and 13,077 in February 2014, an increase of 53 per cent – still a big increase, but nothing like as high as Steve was claiming. Of course, it was technically possible that there had been a huge surge between May 2010 and February 2011 and only a modest increase since then, but that seemed highly improbable.

And the more I thought about it, the more I realised that this increase wasn't as bad news as Steve was implying. It was the result of two things. Rents had increased by more than wages, which clearly *was* bad news, increasing the cost of living for many of my constituents. However, many more people were in work than when Labour left office (unemployment in Croydon was nearly 40 per cent lower than in May 2010), which was surely *good* news. Steve was effectively bemoaning the fact that lots of people had found work and were now earning a salary, but still getting some help with their rent, instead of being out of work and wholly dependent on benefits!

I sent Steve the answer I had received from the House of Commons Library and challenged him to reveal the source of his figures. He sent back a table that he claimed also came from the library (but interestingly not the advice that went with it) and continued to use the 1,100 per cent claim.

In light of his persistence, I went back to the library to see if I could find out what was going on. The reply I received revealed exactly what had happened:

> Dear Mr Barwell,
>
> Thanks for your query. As you may have seen in the table I originally sent you in May, I left out the figures for HB claimants in employment in Croydon Borough over the period November 2008 to October 2010

> as the data published by the DWP for the borough over this period for this category of claimant appear to be wrong. This apparent error also affects Fareham, Uttlesford and Pendle local authorities over the same period – the numbers in employment appear to have been substantially under-estimated in these four areas. This is presumably due to inaccurate recording of claimants' employment status by these local authorities during the period up to and including October 2010. The figure of 1,051 HB claimants in employment in Croydon in May 2010 shown in the table forwarded by Mr Reed is the official figure published by the DWP, but I would suggest that it be treated with caution for the aforementioned reason.
>
> The attached Excel figures update the table I sent you (we now have data for March–May 2014) and highlights the months in which the Croydon borough data shows a discrepancy compared with subsequent months.
>
> I hope this helps – do let me know if you need anything further.

When I looked at the spreadsheet, it was obvious that there was an error in the data. The number of people in work and claiming housing benefit jumped from 1,226 in October 2010 to 8,149 a month later! I suspect that Steve would have been warned about this when the House of Commons Library originally gave him the data. As you can tell from their advice above, their responses to MPs' requests are invariably incredibly thorough. However, since Steve continued to refuse to publish the advice, I couldn't prove that.

I sent this answer on to Steve, copying in journalists from both our local papers so that if he tried to use this figure again in Croydon they would be aware of the facts. I also made it clear to him that if he used the figure again in the House I would raise a point of order to correct the record.

That finally put a stop to it.

Long-term unemployment

On 17 November, the London Labour Party issued the following press release:

Number of long-term unemployed adults in Croydon Central soars 1,000 per cent since last general election

Analysis of the latest official figures from the Office for National Statistics has revealed the total number of adults out of work for more than two years in Croydon Central has rocketed by 1,000 per cent since the last general election.

The figures also show the number of young people signing on for longer than twelve months is up by 300 per cent in just four years ...

Jon Ashworth MP, Labour's shadow Cabinet Office minister, said:

'Like so many of Britain's towns and suburbs, Croydon has so much going for it, but it is being badly let down by its Tory MP and the Tory-led government. We'll be rolling into town to campaign against the devastating rise in long-term unemployment the area has seen in just four years. Sarah Jones, Gloria [De Piero] and I will be talking to Croydon residents on the doorsteps to listen to their concerns and we'll be discussing Labour's positive plan to tackle long-term unemployment and find work for jobless people here.'

Gloria De Piero MP, Labour's shadow Minister for Women and Equalities, added:

'The Tory MP might be oblivious to what's going on here, but with a Labour government and Sarah Jones on Croydon's side folk won't just be left on the dole' ...

Sarah Jones, Labour's parliamentary candidate for Croydon Central, said:

'We need to do all that we can to highlight just what a rough deal Croydon residents have had since 2010, so I'm grateful to have two brilliant campaigning MPs joining me on Tuesday. Gavin Barwell and the Tories have been woefully complacent since they came to power.

> Labour's jobs guarantee would change the lives of people in Croydon who have been left behind by Barwell and this Tory government.'

Once again, these figures felt wrong. Unemployment in my constituency had fallen by nearly 45 per cent under the coalition government: how could long-term unemployment have increased by 1,000 per cent at the same time? It didn't make any sense. So again, I turned to the House of Commons Library to find out the facts. This is the reply I received:

> Dear Mr Barwell,
>
> You asked why the long-term Jobseekers Allowance (JSA) claimant count has increased since May 2010. Since 2010, changes in the way benefits are paid to certain individuals on welfare-to-work programmes have affected the number of long-term claimants of JSA, particularly for young people. Previously, some individuals were moved from claiming JSA onto a Training Allowance when on certain schemes; once they finished the scheme they returned to JSA (if they remained unemployed) but were counted as a new claimant, thereby breaking the original claim's duration. Since 2011, many fewer people have been moved from JSA to a Training Allowance. This has resulted in the statistics showing a higher number of longer-term JSA claimants. A DWP note, 'The effect of policy changes on the youth claimant count', gives more details.
>
> I hope this helps – let me know if you need anything else.

In other words, the Labour government had made it almost impossible for anyone to be counted as long-term unemployed even though lots of people went years without having a job. This was a press release that Alastair Campbell would have been proud of. Make no mention of the fact that unemployment in Croydon Central was down by 45 per cent or that youth unemployment was down by 50 per cent. Instead make a comparison on long-term unemployment that is technically true, but only because your party used to massage the figures.

Anyhow, contrary to what Gloria De Piero claimed, the Tory MP wasn't oblivious to what was going on. When Sarah Jones used these figures at our first hustings meeting, I explained to the audience why this was a highly misleading claim. To be fair to Sarah, judging by her reaction she had no idea the figures were suspect. She certainly never used them again.

These are just two examples, but they illustrate the point. Rebutting false claims is time consuming. There is a risk that the public will see it as petty squabbling. However, it's important that the local media see that you are winning the intellectual battle. And if you keep at it, your opponents will become increasingly nervous about trying it on.

Chapter 10

Friendly fire

RECRUITMENT AND FUNDRAISING were going well, canvassing and the tours of the Palace of Westminster were underway and we were challenging false claims by our opponents, but before we could formally launch the campaign we were struck by what Harold Macmillan referred to as 'events dear boy, events'.

Defection distraction

UKIP had got over 15 per cent in the 2014 council elections, which fortuitously for them had been held on the same day as the European elections. I told myself that had to be their high-water mark. With the European elections out of the way, surely they were going to find it very difficult to stay in the news?

Then, on 28 August, Douglas Carswell, the Conservative MP

for Clacton, announced that he was defecting to UKIP. This was a big surprise. Douglas was certainly a strong Eurosceptic and had in the past been a persistent rebel, but he was what whips refer to as 'an improving stock' – he'd recently announced that with the general election approaching he would be supporting the government and urged other rebels to do the same.

His defection was also a major blow. It wasn't just the loss of an MP. As well as defecting, Douglas had resigned his seat, triggering a by-election to allow his constituents to decide whether they backed his decision to switch to UKIP. He was a good local MP so there was a good chance he would win the by-election. Nonetheless the Conservative Party couldn't be seen to give up on the seat, so we would have to run an energetic campaign. Along with every other Conservative MP, I would be asked to spend precious time in Clacton when I needed to be spending all my time in Croydon.

Self-inflicted wound

If Douglas's defection was a distraction, we were about to be hit by a bombshell.

On 3 September, Croydon Council published data showing how much each councillor had been paid in allowances during the previous financial year. It published such data every September and normally it was a non-event. This year, however, the data showed that Mike Fisher, the leader of the Conservative group (and leader of the council for the period these figures related to), had been paid more than anyone expected.

It turned out that at some point during 2013/14 he had told council officers to increase the special responsibility allowance he was paid as leader of the council by £10,000 a year. He hadn't made this pay rise public at the time, presumably because he didn't want it to be an issue in the run-up to the council elections.

He would have known, however, that it would become public in the end. When the data on pay was published in September, someone was bound to notice.

It may strike you as odd that the leader of the council was able to privately instruct officers to increase his allowance. Surely a council's allowances scheme has to be agreed in a public meeting? Indeed it does. The fact that Mike was able to do this was the result of changes made to Croydon Council's allowances scheme back in 2010/11, based on the recommendations of an independent panel. These changes reduced the overall cost of the scheme. The basic allowance that all councillors receive was cut, so most councillors got less. However, those who received an additional special responsibility allowance – such as the leader of the council, Cabinet members and the mayor, who all have to spend more of their time on council business – had this allowance increased by more than the cut in the basic allowance. They were therefore in line for a net increase in their allowances.

The then Conservative administration rightly decided it would be unfair for any councillor to get an increase at a time when the council's staff were having their pay frozen, so those who were entitled to an increase didn't claim it. Legally, however, they were free to ask for the full amount at any time. That is what Mike had done three years later. It was perfectly legal, but that didn't make it right.

I was both angry and disappointed. First, it was clearly wrong for Mike to get a 17 per cent rise when the council's employees, many of whom were not highly paid, were getting just 1 per cent. It played to all the worst stereotypes of politicians – one rule for us, another for everyone else.

Second, it was also wrong to keep this decision private until after the council elections were out of the way. Openness is a core principle of public life. If Mike felt he deserved a higher salary, he should have made the case publicly.

Third, he had misled me about it. On the weekend after the council elections, he and I had a chat about the results and he told me in passing that he was thinking of putting in a backdated claim for the unclaimed allowance. He had given up a well-paid job to become leader of the council and now he was only leader of the opposition he was in a financial hole. I had every sympathy for the position he found himself in, but I counselled him in the strongest possible terms not to take the money – I felt he would do himself grave political damage from which he would find it hard to recover. Now I realised that when we had that conversation he was already being paid the money.

Finally, on a selfish level this revelation wasn't going to damage just Mike's reputation, but my campaign – and indeed Croydon Conservatives as a whole – too. It was a political gift to Labour.

One of the hardest things in politics is when a friend does something wrong. I had known Mike for nearly twenty years. We had always got on well. He had beaten me to become leader of the Conservative group and I had then supported him, first as his Chief Whip and then as Cabinet member for finance. He, in turn, had been a great support when I was selected as our candidate for Croydon Central and during my time as MP. There is a natural human instinct to stick by your friends even when they have erred.

I had to ask myself two simple questions, however. First, could I defend what he had done morally? Could I justify his giving himself a pay rise, but not telling anyone about it before an election? I could not. If Mike had come to me at the time and told me he needed the extra money, I would have advised him against taking it. If he had insisted he had to do it, however, I would have suggested being open about it and cutting some of the other allowances so there was no net cost to the taxpayer. Had he done that, I would have backed him and taken the political hit when the inevitable criticism came. I owed him that much. I couldn't, however, defend him keeping it secret.

The second question was could Mike ride this out? I didn't think so. I was certain the story would do serious damage both to his reputation and to the reputation of Croydon Conservatives as a whole. The MPs' expenses scandal had shown how potent the issue of allowances could be. If he tried to carry on, his actions would be thrown back at him every time he attacked the council for wasting money or trying to keep something secret.

For both these reasons, my private view was that Mike's position was untenable. He needed to go and it would be better, for both the party's sake and his own long-term future, if he stood down quickly rather than trying to hold on and eventually being forced out.

I was being pressed to make a statement, but I hadn't yet spoken to him directly. I needed to tell him what I thought privately before I said it publicly, so I limited myself to saying:

> I am angry about – and feel very let down by – this news.
>
> First, I believe it is wrong for the leader of the council to get a 17 per cent pay rise at a time when the people who work for the council, many of them on quite low salaries, are getting just 1 per cent. Second, I believe it was doubly wrong to keep this decision private until after the council elections were out of the way ...
>
> Some in my party will be angry with me for issuing this statement. But residents rightly expect politicians to put what is right before party loyalty. If we don't make it clear that what Mike has done is wrong, the actions of one individual will tarnish the reputation of the whole party.

We spoke on the phone the next day. He was upset about my statement and other people's reactions. He felt that after all he had done for the party, at some personal cost, he deserved better. I made it clear that I would always be grateful for the support he had given me and that if he had made the decision public at the time I would have backed him even though there would have been a political price to pay. However, I explained why I couldn't support what he had done in keeping it secret and reminded him that he had misled me when we had spoken shortly after the council elections.

It obviously wasn't an easy conversation, but nor was it a heated one. We subsequently agreed to meet the following night at Cllr Phil Thomas's house.

By his own admission, Phil is a fiery character. He is fond of saying he never stabs people in the back; if he's upset with you, you'll know all about it. He was ice cool that night, however. His view was that Mike's position was untenable, but that I had been wrong to issue a statement. We needed to sort things out behind closed doors and present a united front to the outside world.

Mike quickly accepted he was going to have to go as group leader and we worked on a joint statement to announce that he was standing down. I had learnt from watching countless Westminster scandals at close quarters that the key to handling such events is to get all the facts out in one go. So that's what we did, including revealing that four other Conservative councillors had looked into claiming the additional allowance, but hadn't subsequently done so. Mike's deputies, Dudley Mead and Tim Pollard, and I made it clear that we believed it was necessary for Mike to stand down, but paid tribute to his work for the town.

I want to do so again now. In the eight years Mike Fisher led Croydon Council, school standards rose, recycling soared and council tax bills fell in real terms. He helped the borough recover from the 2011 riots and the 2014 floods and he deserves much of the credit for bringing Westfield and Hammerson to Croydon. His decision to claim the extra money without being open about it was a serious error of judgement, but he has paid for it and he still has a lot to offer to our town.

Politically, Mike standing down and the accompanying statement killed the story. I used my regular email bulletin to make sure as many of my constituents as possible knew the facts before Labour could get a leaflet out. Labour set up an inquiry to try to keep the story running, but it didn't uncover anything new.

It was an unpleasant episode, but we had dealt with it about as well as we could have done. Now we were clear for launch.

Chapter 11

First off the blocks

A vision for Croydon

Back in June 2014 when we agreed our strategy to win Croydon Central, we decided to produce a detailed manifesto and have a high-profile launch to show the Labour Party that we meant business.

Taking these decisions was one thing, implementing them was something else. Doing both properly would involve a lot of work at a time when we were already working hard canvassing, recruiting new activists and raising the money to pay for the campaign. It needed to be done, though. Jason Cummings and Ian Parker agreed to lead on organising the launch, while I would lead on the production of the manifesto.

There is a fundamental problem with producing a local manifesto for a general election campaign: MPs don't run local public services and, if their party is in opposition nationally, they can't influence government policy much either. This meant I couldn't make firm promises. All I could do was produce my vision for the future of the town, setting out what I would try to achieve over the following five years, working with Croydon Council (Labour-controlled until May 2018, but who knew after that?), the Mayor of London (Boris Johnson until May 2016, but who knew after that?) and whichever party or parties formed the next government. There were a lot of unknowns here, but such is the nature of politics. If you can't work with people from other parties when the need arises, you won't get much done.

I approached Chris Philp and Vidhi Mohan, our candidates in Croydon South and Croydon North respectively, to see if they were interested in publishing a joint vision. They were both very happy to do so. Realistically, however, most of the work would fall to me: both of them had full-time jobs outside politics and Chris had only been selected seven months before.

I spent the summer writing and rewriting. Chris and Vidhi then gave me their comments, as well as adding sections specific to Croydon South and Croydon North. The final document was about 20,000 words long. People might not agree with all of its prescriptions, they might not even get all the way to the end, but you couldn't deny it was a comprehensive piece of work.

The document, entitled 'Our Vision for Croydon', started with an honest evaluation of Croydon's strengths and weaknesses. For those who don't know it, or know it only by its (in my view unfair) reputation, Croydon has the potential to be one of the best places in the country to live. It's part of what I think is the greatest city in the world, but on the edge of the beautiful North Downs countryside. It's one of London's greenest boroughs. And it's not just some dormitory suburb feeding London a daily diet of commuters – it's a major office and retail centre in its own right. It's cheaper to live or run a business here than in most other parts of the capital and quicker and easier to get into central London. When I'm out in central London in the early hours of the morning, friends are often amazed that I can still get a train home all through the night, whereas they have to get a cab or night bus. And with people from all over the world having chosen to make our town their home, it's a vibrant, cosmopolitan place to live.

On the other hand, there's a reason the phrase 'as lovely as Croydon' has yet to catch on. First and foremost, the town has an image problem, which the 2011 riots made worse. It's partly a problem of perception – Croydon has a lot more going for it than most people think – but there are real issues we need to address too. The town centre, which is what most people picture when they think of Croydon, is a pretty unattractive place, full of flyovers, underpasses and brutalist 1960s architecture. A number of our district centres are also desperately in need of investment. Our local economy hasn't performed as strongly as other parts of London over the last twenty-five years, which is why the town centre looks so dated.

Our population is growing rapidly and our infrastructure is struggling to keep up. Like many outer London boroughs, we don't get a fair share of various national budgets so public services are stretched. There is significant inequality, with the north of the borough very similar to inner London boroughs like Lambeth, Lewisham and Southwark, but the south very similar to the affluent commuter towns of Surrey.

Finally, we have what I think is an unhealthy political culture. Croydon is a two-party state. There isn't a single Liberal Democrat, Green, UKIP or independent MP or councillor. At a borough-wide level, the two parties are evenly matched. In the 2014 council elections, Labour got 36.3 per cent of the vote to our 33.7 per cent. Four years previously, we received 36.8 per cent to Labour's 31.5 per cent. This tightly contested, two-party system makes for very tribal and often ill-tempered politics. What makes it worse is that both parties' support is heavily geographically concentrated. The north of the borough is a Labour fiefdom, the south is true blue. When Labour are in charge, people in the south feel that they don't get a look in; when we're in charge, people in the north feel the same. In many ways, it's like national politics, but without the smaller parties.

So how did we propose to address these problems? The manifesto set out what we hoped to do:

A stronger local economy

1. Deliver Westfield and Hammerson's proposed redevelopment of the Whitgift shopping centre as quickly as possible. Not only would this create thousands of jobs and transform our retail centre, it would help change Croydon's image, encouraging others to invest here.

2. Offer small and medium-sized businesses tax incentives to relocate here.

3. Transform public spaces in the town centre to make it a much more attractive place to live, work or visit.

4. Tackle litter and fly-tipping by prosecuting those responsible rather than just cleaning up after them.

5. Regenerate our district centres.

6. Work to open a campus of Roehampton University in Croydon (we're the largest town in the country without a university). Not only would this be good for students who wanted to study locally, it would also boost key sectors of our local economy.

7. Raise standards in our schools so that every child – apart from those with a significant learning difficulty – gets at least a C grade in English and maths and hopefully much better. If we want businesses to locate in Croydon, we have to make sure local people have the skills employers want.

Improved infrastructure to cope with population growth

1. Build more homes, but in the right places. There's no need to develop our precious green spaces when we have so many brownfield sites in Croydon.

2. Oppose Labour's plan to make private landlords pay a £200 a year tax on every property they rent out, which would reduce the supply of private rented accommodation and penalise good landlords as well as bad.

3. Secure funding from the government to help Croydon Council provide sufficient school places.

4. Secure funding from the government for a new larger A&E department at Croydon University Hospital and campaign for an urgent care centre at Purley Hospital.

5. Improve the A23, Croydon's key link to the motorway network.

6. Increase capacity and improve reliability on rail services to London Bridge and Victoria and improve key stations like East Croydon.

7. Increase capacity on, and extend, our tram system.

Better public services

1. Secure fairer funding from the government for our schools, the NHS in Croydon and Croydon Council.

2. Raise standards at Croydon University Hospital.

3. Ensure mental health is given the priority it deserves.

4. Renovate our local arts centre, the Fairfield Halls, so that it can put on a wider range of events.

5. Refurbish leisure centres in New Addington and Purley and build a new leisure centre in the town centre.

6. Improve facilities at one of our major parks so that it compares with somewhere like Battersea Park or the new Queen Elizabeth Olympic Park.

A fairer society

1. Give parents a wider choice of schools – hopefully including one or more grammar schools – to drive up standards so that all children, whatever their background, get a good education.

2. Set up a mentoring scheme to help bright children from families where no one has gone to university before achieve their potential.

3. Reform stop-and-search to increase community confidence in the police.

4. Increase the amount of time you have to have lived in the country before you get on the waiting list for council housing.

5. Negotiate a 'City Deal' with the government, giving the council control over some welfare spending so we can use it to transform people's lives, not just help them make ends meet.

A healthier political culture

Work with those from other parties where we agree, be civil where we disagree and think about the needs of the borough as a whole rather than pitting one part of it against another.

You can read the full document at http://issuu.com/gavinbarwellmp/docs/visionforcroydon.

In the end, 'Our Vision for Croydon' was published on 15 September, a week before the launch – that way, the local papers would cover the manifesto one week and the launch the next. We produced an A3 summary, which we distributed to every home in the constituency (see pages 250–51). Labour took one look, presumably decided they couldn't produce something as comprehensive and announced that they wouldn't be producing a manifesto at all. It was a complete reversal from the council election campaign.

A launch like no other

Preparations were now well underway for the launch on 22 September.

We'd distributed a letter from Boris Johnson to every home in the constituency, except those we knew were opposition supporters, inviting anyone who shared his view that I was a great local MP to come to the launch. Over 400 people had said they were coming.

Given the size of the audience, we'd hired the Arnhem Gallery at the Fairfield Halls. We spent a lot of money on a professional set design as well as #BackBarwell2015 T-shirts and badges. It was probably the glitziest launch of an individual constituency campaign British politics has ever seen (an admittedly low bar).

We decided to start the evening with a short video, setting out who I am and what motivates me. Producing this proved to be the most stressful element of the whole event.

I asked Tim Pollard to produce a first draft of the script. When I saw it, I didn't think it was quite right so I made some amendments or, as Tim's version of events would have it, completely rewrote it. After he'd read my redraft he called me up. He sounded rather cross. I apologised for making lots of amendments, but said that given this video was about me and what motivates me, the language needed to be mine. Tim countered that what I had written was way too long, that I didn't know the first thing about writing video scripts and that if I wanted it to be in my words maybe I shouldn't have asked him to do it in the first place. Valid points all. Hopefully the end result benefited from this creative tension.

You can watch the video at www.gavinbarwell.com/videos. I start by talking about how I'm not like many MPs: 'Most MPs aren't from the place they represent. I'm different. I live here. I have done since I was a few months old.' Then I talk about my upbringing and why I am so passionate about education:

> In my work as an MP, I see the terrible environments in which some children grow up – neglected or even abused by the people who should care for them – and I realise how lucky I was.
>
> I had two loving parents who doted on my brother and me. Both Mum and Dad left school at sixteen. They were determined that we would have the opportunities they had missed out on. With their support, I managed to get a scholarship to Trinity School, meaning I could go there without my parents having to pay any fees. Everything I have achieved since is down to the start I had in life from my parents and the fantastic all-round education I got at Trinity.

> That's why I am so passionate about education. I want all young people in Croydon to go to a great school like I did.

I also talk about my friends, who've known me since I was eleven years old, and my wife Karen and our three boys:[13]

> But I got more from Trinity than just a great education. I also made lifelong friends there. Along with my family, they are the most important people in my life. If you're not careful, being an MP can go to your head. My friends have known me for over thirty years. They don't treat me any differently now I am an MP. I know I can rely on them to make sure I don't forget who I am and where I came from ...
>
> I've had one other huge slice of luck in my life and that was meeting my wife, Karen. Like me, she grew up in Croydon. She works for the NHS as a speech and language therapist at Applegarth Primary Academy in New Addington and at Woodside Health Centre. I couldn't do what I do without her support. We now have three sons: Jack, who's just started at secondary school, and Sam and Jamie, who go the local primary school.

I pay tribute to the NHS, which has always been there when my family needed it:

> Although I have been lucky in so many ways, life hasn't always been plain sailing. When I was seven I was diagnosed with cancer. I'm still here because of the NHS. It's not perfect, but the principle – that if you get sick or hurt you don't have to worry whether you can afford treatment – is one of the best things about this country.

---

13 Any politician will tell you that one of the toughest decisions to take in a campaign is how much to talk about your family. Voters are understandably interested in who you are, but say too much and you can't then ask the media to respect your family's privacy. I limited myself to using a short clip of the five of us at a local park for this video and a photo of the same for use in my literature. Towards the end of the campaign, the *Croydon Advertiser* pushed me quite hard for an interview with Karen. She understandably didn't want to do it – after all, she wasn't running for election – so I stood my ground and said no.

> And when I was in my twenties our family had to rely on the NHS again as my dad started to suffer from dementia. Watching him being taken away from us piece by piece was the toughest thing I have ever been through. We will be forever grateful to the NHS and charities like Croydon Crossroads and the Alzheimer's Society that supported us in those difficult times.

And I end by explaining what the campaign is about:

> I'm proud of what I have achieved over the last four and a half years, but there's so much more to do to make Croydon the place we want it to be.
>
> That's why I am standing for re-election. I am launching my campaign tonight, but this evening isn't just about me. It's about Croydon, the great future it can have if we make the right choices. And it's about other people who are working with me to change Croydon for the better – some of whom you are about to hear from.

After the video, some of the amazing people I was working with to change Croydon for the better gave short presentations about what they were doing: John Burton, Westfield's director of development; Jonny Rose from Croydon Tech City, a group of people who have come together to inspire and champion tech business, skills and opportunities in the borough; Eliza Rebeiro from Lives Not Knives, a local charity which she founded to make people aware of the dangers of knife crime, but which now also helps young people into education, training and the world of work; Maureen Martin and Azhar Chaudry, the executive principal and head boy respectively of Quest Academy, one of the fastest-improving schools in the borough; and Rosina St James from The Challenge, who run the National Citizen Service in Croydon.

We had announced their names a few days beforehand. Labour were furious. They too worked closely with a number of these people and didn't appreciate them 'taking sides'. They got council officers to call them to say that if they didn't pull out it would damage their relationship with the council. I was touched that every single one of them refused to be bullied in this way. They weren't coming to the launch to tell people to vote for me; they were coming to talk about the work we were doing together for Croydon.

The next speaker, however, was there to endorse me: the Mayor of London, Boris Johnson.

> I contend that your MP, Gavin Barwell, well, is absolutely fantastic. His energy and his commitment to the Westfield/Hammerson deal was vital. So folks, we want him here in Croydon, don't we? We want him here in Croydon and I'll tell you what else, we want him in Westminster! He's a fantastic local MP, but he's also made some fantastic contributions to the deliberations of that place.

Finally, it was my turn. Following Boris is not easy! I was never going to match him in the humour stakes, so I gave quite a serious speech setting out the challenges Croydon faced. My tone, however, was optimistic:

> If it's wrong to try to gloss over [the problems Croydon faces], it's equally wrong to despair. One of the most depressing things about my job is occasionally meeting constituents who have given up on Croydon. They think it's gone to the dogs and there's nothing that can be done about it.
>
> They're wrong. Over the last few years, we've begun to turn things round.
>
> The number of people in the borough claiming Jobseeker's Allowance is down by 40 per cent since this government came to office. As you've heard tonight, Westfield and Hammerson, two of the biggest retail developers in the country, are investing over £1 billion

> to transform our shopping centre and other investors are following in their footsteps. The council is in the middle of a £50 million programme to transform the public spaces in the town centre ... Our infrastructure is being improved. We're getting record levels of funding from the government to build new schools. Capacity on the rail service to London Bridge is being increased and a new northern entrance to East Croydon station was recently opened. Crime is down by nearly 10 per cent in the last year, with big falls in burglary and robbery. And our schools, which used to be worse than the national average, are now better and improving more quickly.
>
> My key message tonight is that Croydon's best days are ahead of us, not behind. We can reverse the decline. In fact, we can do better than that. We can make our town one of the best places in the country to live. Part of the greatest city in the world, but far greener than most other parts of London. An affordable place to live and work – at least by London standards – with amazing transport connections twenty-four hours a day to central London. Not some dormitory suburb, but a place in its own right with a strong local economy, great public services and all the shops, restaurants, bars, clubs and cultural facilities you could wish for. And home to the most amazing mix of people who live happily side by side, an example to the rest of the world that religion and skin colour need not divide us.

I went on to explain what the election was about:

> It's not a beauty contest – which is lucky for me, because I'd be in real trouble if it was. It's a battle of ideas, what policies we need to pursue to make Croydon the place we all want it to be.
>
> Many of the ideas in our manifesto enjoy cross-party support. That's a good thing. The more we can build consensus about what we need to do to turn Croydon around, the better. Our job between now and 7 May, however, is to explain the areas where our approach differs from Labour's, the choice people face at the next election.

I went on to identify seven key differences – on how to build a strong economy, how to raise standards in our schools, our attitude to crime, our approach to immigration, where to build the new homes we desperately needed, what sort of homes they should be and how to make work pay. I ended by saying that if we won this battle of ideas we could transform Croydon into 'a place that is the envy of people across the country, not the butt of comedians' jokes'.

The launch cost a lot of money. I doubt whether it directly won me one extra vote. It was worth every penny, though, for the effect it had on the morale of our existing activists and the new people it got involved.

We went for a beer afterwards in the Spread Eagle. I was surprised people didn't take off their #BackBarwell2015 T-shirts when we left the Fairfield Halls. This was clearly a campaign people wanted to be associated with. Either that or they didn't have a change of clothes...

Anyhow, #BackBarwell2015 was officially off the ground.

The next key moment in the campaign was one I had no influence over. My prospects in Croydon Central might be dramatically altered by events in Manchester and Birmingham. It was time for the party conferences.

Chapter 12

A tale of two conferences

Anyone who works in politics knows that the last two weeks in September and the first week in October are party conference season. The conferences used to be major gatherings of the political tribes. Nowadays, you'll find more lobbyists and journalists than party activists. Nonetheless, for one week each year each party has the media spotlight focused on it. Most of the time, nothing that is said makes any difference on the frontline, but occasionally a major announcement – or a serious gaffe – changes the political climate.

The peril of speaking without notes

Labour's conference is generally held in the last week of September, the week before ours. Ed Miliband gave his keynote speech on 23 September, the day after my local campaign launch.

His last two conference speeches had gone well. In 2012 he had attempted to claim the 'One Nation' mantle from us in a highly personal and effective speech. To this day, I don't understand why he didn't follow the idea through after the conference. Then in 2013 his promise to freeze energy bills got some traction as well, even if subsequent falls in energy prices made this look not such good politics.

Now he faced a big test: his final conference speech before the general election. This was the one occasion when what he had to say was guaranteed to be the lead story on the six and ten o'clock news bulletins. It was therefore his best chance between now and polling day to change voters' perceptions of him. He tried to repeat the trick of speaking without notes, which had worked so well for him in 2012 and 2013.

This time, it went disastrously wrong. He left out a whole section on immigration and forgot to mention the deficit. As James Forsyth of *The Spectator* asked, 'Were there two worse topics for Ed Miliband to forget?' The biggest concern many floating voters had about Labour was on the economy – could they be trusted to get Britain back into the black or would they spend too much again? Rather than reassure those voters, the Leader of the Opposition had just massively underlined that concern.

The reaction was almost universally bad. A shadow Cabinet member told the *Daily Mail*: 'It was the worst speech by a Labour leader I have ever seen. If he somehow becomes Prime Minister, the party is f*****.' Even Len McCluskey, the leader of the Unite union and a fierce opponent of austerity, said Miliband had made a 'glaring omission'.

Perhaps he was exhausted from the Scottish referendum campaign, which had ended just a few days previously. Whatever the reason, he had missed an opportunity to shift public opinion Labour's way. Could we do any better?

Reckless by name...

If Labour's conference had ended badly, ours got off to the worst possible start. On the eve of the conference, Mark Reckless, the Conservative MP for Rochester & Strood, announced that he was defecting to UKIP and resigning to cause another by-election.

This defection sparked a very different reaction than Douglas Carswell's departure. There was real anger at the way Mark had behaved. There had been rumours that there might be another defection and the Chief Whip spoke to several MPs who we suspected might be considering it. They included Mark, but he gave a categorical assurance that he wasn't going anywhere. A couple of days later, it was clear how much his word was worth.

People also seemed much less sorry to see Mark go than Douglas – he wasn't as popular and people felt he was nowhere near as effective a local MP. There was real hope that we could win the by-election, or at least win the seat back at the general election if we lost the by-election, and make him pay for his treachery.

Retail policies

This was clearly a far from ideal start to conference, but straight away things began to look up as ministers made a series of announcements about what a Conservative majority government would do.

On Saturday, the Prime Minister announced more help for people to buy their first home. This was music to my ears – young people in my constituency were finding it increasingly difficult to get on the housing ladder. If we didn't do something, we were in danger of going to go back to a time when owning your own home was the preserve of a privileged few.

Then on Sunday he signalled that a Conservative government would reduce immigration from the EU. This would also be popular in my constituency. Most of my constituents aren't anti-immigration. Many are migrants themselves or the children of migrants, and those who are not have friends, neighbours or colleagues at work who are. They know from personal experience that most of the people who settle here work hard and make a big contribution to our country. They simply want the overall numbers reduced. My own view was that we were in danger of squeezing immigration from places like India too hard to compensate for the fact that immigration from within the EU was increasing. It was good to hear that we were going to strike a more sensible balance.

On Monday, the Chancellor announced plans to reduce the cap on the amount of benefits an out-of-work family can receive from £26,000 to £23,000 a year. This cap was one of our most popular policies. Under Labour, there had been no cap at all and some out-of-work families had got over £50,000 a year in benefits, far more than most working families earned.

On Tuesday, the Prime Minister announced that a Conservative government would make sure everyone could get access to a GP seven days a week. This was another announcement that would go down well in Croydon – lots of constituents were finding it difficult to get an appointment with their GP.

Finally, in his main conference speech on the Wednesday, the Prime Minister promised to let people keep more of the money they work hard to earn by increasing the personal allowance (the amount you can earn before you start paying income tax) to £12,500 and the higher rate threshold (the amount over which you start paying 40 pence income tax for every pound you earn) to £50,000. When Labour left office in 2010, the personal allowance was just £6,475. We had already increased it to £10,000, making someone earning just £10,000 a year £700 better off than they had been under Labour. Now we would go further still.

The changes to the higher rate threshold were important too. The 40 pence rate was only meant to be paid by the rich, but in recent years more and more people had been dragged into it, particularly in London where wages are higher because the cost of living is higher. Someone living in my constituency who was making £50,000 a year was earning far more than the national average, but given the much higher cost of living they certainly weren't rich. This policy would make them about £100 a month better off.

There were lots of other policies announced, but I suspected most of them would make no difference at the frontline. Here were five, however, on helping people to become home owners, reducing immigration, making the welfare system fairer, improving the NHS and letting people keep more of the money they worked hard to earn that I thought would help me if we could communicate them.

A great speech but who's listening?

The Prime Minister's speech got rave reviews from across the political spectrum. Tom Bradby, ITV's political editor, said it was 'the best speech I have seen David Cameron give in the decade I have been reporting on him'. Rafael Behr from the left-leaning *New Statesman* had to concede that 'he made Miliband and Farage look like small fish'. And Isabel Hardman from the centre-right *Spectator* declared that 'if general elections are won on conference speeches, then David Cameron has just romped to victory'.

Which was all well and good, except general elections are not won on conference speeches. We'd had a better conference than Labour, but how many people would hear about the policy announcements? In Croydon we produced a leaflet, which we distributed to every home in the constituency, to spread the word (see pages 252–3) but how much difference would it make?

Only time would tell.

Chapter 13

Bad news is good news

REMEMBER, REMEMBER THE fifth of November. That was the day on which Michael Ashcroft published the first of his three polls of the Croydon Central electorate.

Michael had stood down as deputy chairman of the Conservative Party with responsibility for polling and target seats shortly after the 2010 election, but he continued to commission polling. Instead of presenting it privately to the Conservative Party, he now began to publish it for anyone to study. Our loss was our opponents' and the political commentators' gain as they suddenly had access to a wealth of information to which previously only we had been privy.

His research consisted of three strands:

1. national polls;

2. focus groups; and

3. polls in the marginal constituencies that were likely to determine the result of the election.

Polls are quantitative research ('quant'). They are designed to provide an accurate measure of what a given group of people think. For a national poll, the research company will normally interview about 1,000 people, which statistically is enough to give a margin of error of plus or minus 3 percentage points 95 per cent of the time.[14] They adjust the raw results so that the sample is representative of both the demographic mix of the group of people being surveyed and, in the case of political polls, the voting patterns at the last election. For example, if only 44 per cent of the people the pollster interviewed were women, it will give more weight to their views because women make up about 52 per cent of the electorate in Great Britain. If 40 per cent of those interviewed claim to have voted Conservative in 2010, the pollster will give less weight to their views because the Conservatives only got 37 per cent of the vote in Great Britain in 2010. Pollsters also adjust the raw results to reflect how likely people say they are to vote – the views of someone who says they are certain to vote will count for more than the views of someone who says they are unlikely to vote.

Focus groups, on the other hand, are qualitative research ('qual'). They are designed to get beneath the headline numbers and find out why people think what they think. The research company will have a much longer discussion with a small group of people.

Michael published his first twenty-six constituency polls in May 2014. They were, as he became fond of saying, 'a snapshot

14 These margins of error mean there is no point getting excited about one poll that shows your party ahead by 3 percentage points. It might have overstated your party's share by 3 percentage points and understated your opponent's share by 3 percentage points; in other words, you might actually be behind by 3 points! Or it might be one of the one in twenty polls that is out by more than 3 percentage points (pollsters call these 'rogue' polls). You need to look at the rolling average of all published opinion polls. This is a lesson that most people who tweet about politics have yet to learn.

not a prediction', but across the twenty-six seats the average swing from the Conservatives to Labour was 6.5 per cent. If there was a swing of this size in every seat in the country, Labour would gain eighty-three seats (including Croydon Central), giving them a comfortable overall majority in the next House of Commons.

Croydon Central was not in the first twenty-six polls, but our turn would come. I waited with some trepidation. That trepidation increased as the results for more and more Conservative/Labour marginals in London were published. We were 8 then 15 points behind in Hendon, 9 then 17 points behind in Hampstead & Kilburn, 13 points behind in Brentford & Isleworth and 10 points behind in Enfield North.

In early November, I got a message from Michael alerting me that a Croydon Central poll was in the field and would be published on the 5th. He promised to send me the headline figures before they became public.

On this occasion, I found my first golden rule (don't worry about things you can't control) difficult to observe. If the poll was very good for me, it might lead Labour HQ to give up on the seat and shift resources elsewhere. It seemed unlikely that it would be *that* good, however. What I was really hoping for was an indication that our hard work since May was having an impact.

When I saw the figures, my hopes were dashed. Michael's polls included two different voting intention questions. The first was, 'If there was a general election tomorrow, which party would you vote for?' Asking the question this way led to the following voting intentions:

Labour	36 per cent
Conservatives	31 per cent
UKIP	23 per cent
Liberal Democrats	4 per cent
Greens	4 per cent

The second question was, 'Thinking specifically about your own parliamentary constituency at the next general election and the candidates who are likely to stand for election to Westminster there, which party's candidate do you think you will vote for in your own constituency?' Asking the question this way led to:

Labour	39 per cent
Conservatives	33 per cent
UKIP	19 per cent
Liberal Democrats	4 per cent
Greens	4 per cent

It was this latter question that Michael and his team felt was likely to be the best indicator of who was going to win. And it wasn't me.

It's worth noting that CCHQ used a different second question in their private polling, which gave the names of the various candidates. I'm told by others (CCHQ never, to my knowledge, did a poll of Croydon Central) that this led to more favourable results for incumbents. CCHQ's argument was that given that candidate names appear on the ballot paper they should be used in the question. Michael's view was that if people had a favourable opinion of one of their local candidates, they shouldn't need to be reminded of their name.

Commenting on the poll, Michael generously observed: 'The six-point Labour lead in Croydon Central is the smallest I have yet found in a seat the Tories are defending from Labour in London.' That was about the most positive spin that could be put on the result. 'It looks like Gavin is going to be looking for a new job' would have been closer to the truth.

I was particularly worried by the fact that Labour did better when people were asked to think about the candidates standing in the seat. We were banking on me having a reasonable personal vote, but this poll suggested that either I didn't have one or, if

I did, it was being outweighed by supporters of smaller parties who, when asked to think about the candidate standing in their seat, were prepared to vote tactically for Labour to stop me winning. Just as bad, UKIP were on 19 per cent, 3.5 percentage points higher than they had polled in the council elections, which I had thought would be their high-water mark. There was simply no way I could win with UKIP doing that well.

There were two more questions that confirmed that we were in a deep hole. The first asked, 'Are there any of the political parties that you would definitely not vote for at the next general election?' Thirty-nine per cent said that they would definitely not vote Labour, but a depressing 48 per cent said that they would definitely not vote Conservative. Despite everything David Cameron had done to change perceptions of the Conservative Party for the better, the job was clearly far from complete. If we couldn't reduce the percentage of the electorate who wouldn't even consider voting Conservative, I was going to have to get nearly all of those who were prepared to consider doing so to actually vote for me if I was to have any chance of winning.

The other question was about what kind of government people wanted to see after 7 May 2015: 'Which of the following would you most like to see as the outcome of the next general election?' This led to the following results:

A Labour government	34 per cent
A Conservative government	27 per cent
A coalition between Labour and the Liberal Democrats	11 per cent
A coalition between the Conservatives and the Liberal Democrats	9 per cent

There was some silver lining, though. Three questions showed signs of an advantage for us.

The first was about the economy: 'Thinking about Britain's economy – including things like jobs, wages, prices, taxes and interest rates – how do you think the British economy will fare over the next year for you and your family?' Sixty-one per cent thought it would fare well; just 35 per cent thought it would fare badly.

The second was about who people preferred as Prime Minister. Thirty per cent were satisfied with the job David Cameron was doing overall as Prime Minister. Twenty-seven per cent were dissatisfied with the job he was doing and would prefer to have Ed Miliband. Crucially, though, 27 per cent were dissatisfied with the job that David Cameron was doing and yet would still prefer to have him as PM than Ed Miliband. Being considered 'not great, but better than that other guy' may not be what any politician aims for, but you take what you can get.

These two results vindicated key elements of our strategy. The people of Croydon Central wanted a Labour government, but they felt we were doing a good job on the economy and they wanted David Cameron to stay as Prime Minister. By 7 May they would have to resolve this paradox. If we could focus them on the choice of Prime Minister, we were still in with a chance.

The third question that offered signs of encouragement was a measure of local activity: 'Have any of the main political parties contacted you over the last few weeks whether by delivering leaflets or newspapers, sending personally addressed letters, emailing, telephoning you at home or knocking on your door?' Fourteen per cent had heard from Labour; 19 per cent had heard from us. At this stage, we were winning the ground war, though the real test was still to come as we approached polling day and Labour began to deploy activists from across south London.

There was also some useful intelligence in the underlying data. Sixty-seven per cent of 2010 Conservative voters were still planning to vote Conservative; 23 per cent were planning to switch to UKIP and 7 per cent to Labour. Eighty-two per cent of 2010 Labour voters were still planning to vote Labour; 9 per cent were planning to switch to me and 6 per cent to UKIP.

This meant that there was virtually no net direct swing from us to Labour (roughly equal numbers of people were switching from us to Labour and from Labour to us). The reason Labour were ahead was the deadly combination of the collapse of the Liberal Democrat vote, most of which was going to Labour (45 per cent of 2010 Liberal Democrats were planning to vote Labour; only 11 per cent were planning to vote for me), and the fact that UKIP were drawing their support much more from former Conservatives than former Labour supporters.

There was one final straw to be clutched at. Surely we could lure some voters back from UKIP and possibly from Labour too, whereas Labour had already squeezed the Liberal Democrat and Green votes as low as they could go?[15]

The question now was how to respond to this bad poll. The standard politician response in this situation is, 'The only poll that counts is the one on polling day', which is code for, 'Oh my God, this looks grim, but if you think I'm going to admit that you can think again.' I favoured a different approach. Rather than make myself look silly by trying to pretend this wasn't bad news, I would admit it. In fact, I'd go further, publicising it in the hope that fear of Labour winning the seat would convince some former Conservatives to come back to us as well as motivating more strong Conservative supporters to offer to help with the campaign. I issued a statement admitting that the poll

> obviously doesn't make for very cheery reading for me ... Hopefully it will help to convince those 2010 Conservative voters tempted to switch to UKIP that if they do so, they'll end up with a Labour MP and in all probability Ed Miliband as Prime Minister. If, like me, you think that would be a disaster for this country and you're prepared to help out to make sure it doesn't happen, get in touch.

---

15 Spoiler alert: we were indeed able to squeeze the UKIP vote, but I was wrong to assume that the Liberal Democrat and Green votes couldn't go any lower.

The beauty of this strategy was that I could rely on some of the more excitable people on the other side reinforcing it by glorying in my imminent demise. Sure enough, the Labour-supporting website Inside Croydon obliged later that day:

> *Grim outlook for Barwell as Ashcroft poll puts him six points down*
> Things are looking very grim for Gavin Barwell's future as an MP, as even his former employer and one-time mentor is publishing figures which show that he will lose his Croydon Central seat at the general election next May.

The strategy did ultimately work. The electorate became increasingly aware that this was a close race and Conservatives toying with the idea of voting UKIP began to say on the doorstep, 'I like what Farage is saying, but I don't want to let Labour in.' People also began to spontaneously contact us offering to help with the campaign.

With six months to go, however, I was still up that creek.

Chapter 14

Prediction addiction

PUBLISHED OPINION POLLS are a mixed blessing. They can provide valuable intelligence about public opinion, which either validates your campaign strategy or suggests ways in which it needs to change. However, they can also be a big distraction, diverting the rival campaigns into arguing about what it all means instead of focusing on what they can do to change the result.

Objectively, I knew I shouldn't pay too much attention to what was a snapshot of public opinion six months before the election with a margin of error of plus or minus 3 percentage points. When it was my future and my chance to continue working for the place I've lived all my life on the line, though, that was easier said than done.

Still, at least the poll was a one-off.

What are my numbers today?

Then Mark Lancaster introduced me to electionforecast.co.uk. Mark sat opposite me in the whips' office. He had been a good source of advice when I was first appointed and was an equally good source of office banter. His seat, Milton Keynes North, wasn't as marginal as mine, but it wasn't a safe seat either so he understood the pressure I was under.

We were chatting about our respective seats one day when he asked what my predicted share of the vote was on the election-forecast website. I didn't know what he was talking about, so he showed me the site.

The moment I saw it, I knew I was going to regret looking at it. The academics behind the site had built a model that used past results, demography and national and constituency polling to predict the result in every constituency in the country and also assess the likelihood of that result. You could click on Croydon Central and it would tell you what share of the vote they thought each candidate was going to get and what percentage chance they thought each of us had of winning. These figures were updated every few days based on the latest published national polls and Ashcroft constituency polls.

The model looked impressive. It was predicting with a reasonable degree of accuracy the results of individual Ashcroft constituency polls. It certainly seemed to be a better predictor of my prospects than the national opinion polls, both because it took account of how the different parties were doing in different parts of the country and because it assumed, based on what had happened in previous elections, that the governing party would recover in the polls as polling day approached.

This was the stuff of nightmares: a prediction of my chances of saving my skin that would be updated every few days and which appeared to be soundly based. I told myself that no good would come from looking at this site, but it proved increasingly impossible to resist. I was an addict.

For the last four or five months of the campaign, these predictions shaped my daily mood. It became a running joke in the whips' office. If I greeted people with a cheery 'Good morning', it meant the latest numbers were good. A monosyllabic grunt meant bad news.

I still blame Mark Lancaster for setting me on the road to becoming a poll data junkie.

Gaffe-prone Gav is gonna lose

There was another source of predictions – the Labour-supporting Inside Croydon website. However, their predictions were more a source of amusement than concern because they were based on their somewhat biased analysis of other people's data, rather than any original information of their own. They were published under the pseudonym Walter Cronxite,[16] but the writing style was clearly that of my predecessor, Andrew Pelling. The first prediction was published on 18 October, before Michael Ashcroft published his poll:

> I predict the Croydon Central result next May as:
>
> Labour 18,750 (37.5 per cent)
> Cons 17,150 (34.3 per cent)
> UKIP 8,300 (16.6 per cent)
> Lib Dems 2,600 (5.2 per cent)
> Greens 2,100 (4.2 per cent)
> Others 1,100 (2.2 per cent)

16 Many Croydoners affectionately refer to their home town as 'The Cronx' – south London's equivalent of the Bronx – so in adopting the pseudonym 'Walter Cronxite' the writer is styling himself as Croydon's equivalent of the legendary US newsreader Walter Cronkite.

They obviously got the outcome wrong, but to be fair the polls and the bookies were all predicting Sarah Jones would win at this point. A fairer test of how good 'Walter' is at predicting elections is to compare the number of votes he predicted each party would get with the final result, which you'll find in Chapter 22.[17]

Inside Croydon continued to predict my demise with unrestrained glee until the final days of the campaign, when they finally caught on that I was in with a chance of winning and hedged their bets. If I did manage to win, the egg on their faces would be an added bonus.

17 Spoiler alert: he's no Nostradamus.

Chapter 15

'Tis the season to petition

A KEY ELEMENT OF our strategy to hold Croydon Central was to maximise my personal vote – the people who wanted me to stay as their local MP even though they weren't naturally Conservative supporters. One way of doing that was running campaigns on local issues. Some MPs don't get involved in such issues, leaving them to local councillors, but from the moment I was elected I felt it was part of my job to use my position to influence the council and other organisations that provide local services to change things in my constituency for the better. As well as being the right thing to do, it was also good politics, showing that I cared about our local area and helping to position me as a different kind of MP.

Labour's victory in May's council elections had been a big blow, but the one upside was that when I campaigned against something the council had done I was no longer opposing my own colleagues. Sarah would now have to wrestle with that dilemma. And it quickly became apparent that the new administration was going to give me lots of issues to campaign on.

Save our school fields

In their manifesto for the council elections, Labour said they viewed open spaces as 'key assets for the local community'. Any reasonable person would interpret that as meaning they believed these places needed to be protected. In November 2014, however, Labour councillors approved a paper entitled 'Asset Strategy 2014–2019', which gave a different meaning to those words. It proposed building on some school fields: 'A number of school sites have very large playing fields and ancillary land that may be considered excessive for the number of students that attend the school. Where this may be the case the schools will be identified and opportunities considered for development of affordable housing.'

When one of our local papers, the *Croydon Advertiser*, challenged the councillor responsible for this policy, Simon Hall, he admitted that a list had been drawn up of all schools in Croydon comparing pupil numbers with playing field size but 'he was reluctant to give specific examples'. When pushed, he admitted 'some are in the New Addington area' and finally named one, Castle Hill Primary in his own Fieldway ward.

I considered this an appalling policy. There are plenty of brownfield sites in Croydon suitable for development. What we're short of – particularly in the centre and north of the borough – is open spaces. Yet at a time when more and more children weren't getting enough exercise, our council was planning to build on their playing fields.

I was confident that most of the people I represented, whatever their political views, would feel the same way. I therefore launched a petition to try to get the council to think again. As well as emailing it to everyone I had an address for, we collected signatures at pick-up time outside the schools most likely to be affected. Thousands of people signed. I also submitted a Freedom of Information request to the council to try to get hold of the list which Cllr Hall had mentioned to the *Croydon Advertiser*.

I wanted to make this a cross-party campaign, so I invited my Labour, Liberal Democrat, Green and UKIP equivalents to join me in lobbying to get the policy changed. Most agreed to do so, but Labour's Sarah Jones refused to say what her view was. She was in a difficult position – agreeing with me would have put her at odds with the Labour council – but dealing with difficult positions is part of the job she aspired to.

The council's reaction was beyond parody. Stage one was denial. There was no plan to build on school playing fields. I was making it up. It didn't matter what 'Asset Strategy 2014–2019' said (it rapidly became clear that, apart from Cllr Hall, none of the other councillors who had approved this paper had actually read it). The council responded to my Freedom of Information request denying that a list comparing the size of school sites with pupil numbers had ever been drawn up, effectively accusing Cllr Hall of being a liar or a fantasist.

This line collapsed rather rapidly. A council meeting on Monday 1 December ended in farce when Labour councillors voted en masse against a Conservative motion to remove references to building on school playing fields from 'Asset Strategy 2014–2019', despite saying they had no plans to build on school playing fields. Under pressure during the council meeting, Cllr Hall made the mistake of accusing the *Advertiser* of misquoting him. The *Advertiser* then published the full transcript of the interview, which revealed that Cllr Hall hadn't been misquoted at all – in fact, he had gone on at some length about reviewing the size of each school site and the need to free up land to build more housing.

Stage two was the inevitable U-turn. On 2 December, the leader of the council, Councillor Tony Newman, decided to remove the paragraph I had been quoting from 'Asset Strategy 2014–2019'. He didn't bring the document back to a public meeting to approve the change, however – that would have been rather embarrassing. Instead, he used his executive power to amend it in private (if policies can be signed off in private, it makes you wonder why councils bother to agree them in public, doesn't it?). He still didn't seem to have read the whole document, though. He took out the paragraph I had been quoting, but left in two others that said the same thing. Even if the document still contained references to building on school playing fields, however, it was clear that the policy was now dead.

With panto season underway, the *Advertiser* came up with a fantastic front page mocking the council's twists and turns under the headline 'Spinderella'. Even the normally Labour-supporting Inside Croydon described the council's handling of the issue as 'an unedifying clusterf***'.

£25,000 of M&S vouchers to be won
FULL DETAILS PAGE 37
Christmas unwrapped

CROYDON ADVERTISER
local news all day every day @ croydonadvertiser.co.uk

INSIDE...
Teenagers convicted of stabbing
Outlet boss promises a better store
X Factor final looms for Ben

Spin-derella

WE MIGHT BUILD ON PLAYING FIELDS
OH NO WE WON'T

Report, supported by cabinet member, said council would look at **building on school playing fields**
■ Councillors take to Twitter to **deny policy** despite approving document
■ They reject public call to amend report only for council leader to do it **behind closed doors**

A pantomime farce starring Croydon Council... FULL STORY:

Croydon Coaches
Calais
Blackbushe Sunday Market
020 8763 0077
www.croydoncoaches.org.uk

The *Advertiser* front page on the pantomime farce that was the council's school playing fields policy

There were several lessons to be learnt from this. First, the Labour administration didn't seem to be thinking things through before agreeing them and was therefore liable to U-turn if enough people complained about something. Second, it was clear that given the size of my email database and people's willingness to forward emails to their friends and neighbours, I was quickly able to get a large number of people to complain without too much work on my part. And third, because people were forwarding the emails to friends and neighbours, a by-product of the campaign had been that I had grown the size of my email database.

It had been a win–win and was surely worth repeating.

A bridge to nowhere

Buoyed by my success on school fields, in early December I launched my next campaign.

In December 2013, Network Rail had opened a much-needed new northern entrance to East Croydon station to relieve pressure on the main ticket hall. There was an exit on one side of the tracks and a plan that property developer Menta would build a link across the site they were developing on the other side as well. This would allow people living in the Addiscombe area to access the new entrance and create a handy pedestrian route across the railway.

Nearly one year later, nothing had happened. The bridge Network Rail had built across the railway ended in a dead end on one side and Addiscombe residents were still having to walk in a big loop to get a train, all for the want of a route across a ten-metre strip of land. The previous Conservative administration had promised to build a temporary link across Menta's land, but the new Labour administration told me that they couldn't afford to do anything and residents would have to wait until Menta had developed their site 'circa 2019/20'.

I felt that was unreasonable so I launched a petition calling on the council and Network Rail to open a temporary link as soon as possible. Once again, I sent it out to everyone on my email list and also spent a freezing morning outside East Croydon station handing out flyers. And once again, thousands of people signed.

This time, however, there was no happy ending. Both the council and Network Rail accepted something must be done, but they couldn't agree on what or who should fund it. I'm still pursuing the issue today.

Green Belt guardian

The next petition followed only a week later. This one wasn't my idea. I was approached by Addington Residents' Association about protecting some green fields in their area from development. They had been contacted by representatives of Persimmon Homes, who had added the land to their list of potential sites. It seemed Persimmon thought they had a chance of getting planning permission from Croydon Council, even though the land was part of the Green Belt.

Addington Residents' Association had written to the leader of the council asking for an assurance that any planning application would be rejected. To be fair to him, there was no way he could give that. Councils have a quasi-judicial role when determining planning applications, so they mustn't be seen to have made their minds up about a scheme before it comes to them for decision. He could, however, have offered to meet Persimmon, explain to them that there was a strong presumption against development in the Green Belt in the council's planning policies and encourage them to look at other, more suitable sites in the borough. Instead, he sent a response that offered very little reassurance. Coupled with the statement by Sarah Jones that the council needed to 'be brave and build in places people might not want us to', you could understand why the Residents' Association was worried.

We agreed to launch a petition to show Persimmon and the council the strength of feeling locally about these fields, which formed a vital green corridor separating Addington and New Addington. Hopefully, this would dissuade Persimmon from even submitting an application. Again we got a great response and to date there's been no sign of an application.

New Addington recycling centre

A week later, Cllr Alison Butler, the deputy leader of Croydon Council, revealed that the council was looking to close Fishers Farm recycling centre in New Addington. She told the *Advertiser*: 'We are looking to use the ... land because it overlooks a lot of green and open sites and would be a good location for a housing scheme.'

There was no mention of providing a replacement recycling centre somewhere else in the local area. That really worried me. It was a long way to the nearest alternative recycling centre and even with Fishers Farm nearby there was already a big problem with fly-tipping in the area. Closing the centre was bound to make things worse.

So I launched another petition calling on the council to keep Fishers Farm open or, failing that, replace it with a new recycling centre somewhere else in the area. Again, large numbers of people signed and again we achieved a positive result. The council promised that if it closes Fishers Farm a new recycling centre 'will be re-provided locally pre-closure'.

The Advertiser strikes back

The *Croydon Advertiser* decided it was time to take me to task for launching so many campaigns in such a short space of time. On 19 December, they launched what they called 'The Campaign to End All Campaigns', calling on me to stop launching campaigns:

> 'Gavin, we get it, there's an election on,' said an *Advertiser* spokesman. Mr Barwell's quest to break a world record for pre-election campaigning began on 10 November ... This week, Mr Barwell set up a fifth petition ... In contrast Sarah Jones, Labour's prospective candidate for Croydon Central, is lagging behind with just one campaign – for East and West Croydon stations to be moved from zone 5 to 4. Not one to pass up an opportunity, Mr Barwell has got in on the act and publicly backed that idea too.
>
> Unconvinced the former Coulsdon West councillor can go cold turkey this Christmas, the *Advertiser* is calling on residents fed up of being asked to sign petitions to sign a petition calling on Mr Barwell to stop setting up petitions. Sign up below, no email address required.

I thought this was a great pre-Christmas story. It was a fair cop, but done in a light-hearted way and it was hardly bad publicity – I was being criticised for working too hard!

That wasn't the end of it, however. In the New Year, the BBC's *Daily Politics* show was looking to do a piece about how everyone was already fed up with the general election campaign. They thought the *Advertiser* story was a great example, so they interviewed me and the then editor of the *Advertiser*, Glenn Ebrey. It was like my own party-political broadcast. Jo Coburn asked me how I responded to the charge that I was working hard to try to keep my job. I replied:

> I'm guilty as charged. I've been working hard for the four and a half years that I've represented the seat ... The *Advertiser* has said in previous editorials that whether you agree with my views or not you can't doubt my commitment to Croydon ... I'm very lucky because I represent my home town in Parliament. Very few MPs get to do that. I love this job. There is so much to do to make Croydon the place it could be.

I even got an opportunity to pay tribute to my tormentor: 'Some of the campaigns that I've run ... I've actually run with the *Advertiser*.

It's a great local campaigning paper ... we worked together on the campaign to get Lillian's Law to tighten up the law in relation to drug driving.'

Jo ended by asking Glenn if he'd received any complaints from readers about me running all these campaigns. He laughed and replied, 'Er, no.'

'I don't think you're going to stop Gavin Barwell from campaigning,' she said.

Indeed.

Chapter 16

New Year Blue

An enforced rest

I HAD AN ENFORCED rest over the Christmas and New Year holiday. The bit of me that had lost all sense of proportion found it very difficult to stop, but fortunately the rational bit that was still left recognised that knocking on people's doors at this time of year would cost rather than win me votes.

The break did me good – the pressure and the lack of a decent night's sleep had been taking their toll. It was great to spend some quality time with Karen and the kids for the first time in twelve months (we'd not had a proper summer holiday because I had been working so hard on the campaign). After this, though, I knew there would be no more breaks before polling day. I needed to think about how I was going to get through the next four and a bit months.

I decided to make two small changes to my lifestyle. First, I tried to go for a short walk during the day on weekdays to make sure I saw some daylight (at this time of year, it was dark when I arrived at work and dark when I left). Second, I pretty much stopped drinking alcohol. I'm not a heavy drinker in any case, but I found that whereas I normally enjoyed a few pints with my mates it was now making me feel a bit down, not the outcome you want from a night out.

It's hardly cutting-edge health advice, but these two changes made the marathon slog that was to come easier to bear.

Optimistic for Croydon

I may have been struggling in the polls, but 2015 looked like being a great year for Croydon. I set out why in my first email bulletin of the year:

> I am by nature one of life's optimists, but even discounting for that it's hard not to be hopeful about 2015.
>
> There are already cranes up all over the town centre – Saffron Square, Taberner House, Cherry Orchard Road, even the Gateway site next to East Croydon that has lain vacant for my entire life.
>
> In February, we have the public inquiry to determine whether Croydon Council will be granted a Compulsory Purchase Order for the remaining parts of the Westfield/Hammerson site. The result is expected around July and if, as I hope and expect, it's a yes then work can finally get underway.
>
> And there is plenty of other good news in the pipeline. Work should also get underway on the regeneration of Central Parade, New Addington. Our schools and local NHS will be getting above-inflation increases in funding in April because this government has changed the unfair systems for allocating funds between different parts of the country that it inherited from the previous government.

We're waiting for a decision about funding for a new accident and emergency department at Croydon University Hospital. We're negotiating a growth deal with the government that should provide the funding for the extra infrastructure we need to support the regeneration of Croydon. And I hope the council will bring some much-needed investment to Portland Road and listen to the hundreds of people who have signed my petition calling for a link from Cherry Orchard Road to the new northern entrance to East Croydon station.

Nationally, our economy is growing strongly – more strongly than any other advanced economy. It is creating jobs at a record rate – unemployment is falling faster than at any time since records began (here in Croydon Central, it's halved since this government came to office). The deficit – measured as a percentage of our national output – has been halved. Inflation is falling. And wages are finally rising faster than the rate of inflation.

These aren't dry statistics. They mean that this time next year most of us will be better off; hundreds of thousands of people who are currently out of work will have a job and be able to provide for their families; and we will be a step closer to eliminating the deficit and getting back in the black.

Things aren't perfect of course – there are still far too many people who don't have a job or don't get paid enough to have a decent quality of life. But on virtually every measure we are moving in the right direction.

It was difficult for Sarah Jones to dispute any of this – economically things *were* headed in the right direction. If I could just keep the focus on the economy, I should be OK. Once again, however, events intervened.

An A&E crisis?

At 7 a.m. on 6 January, Croydon University Hospital (CUH) declared an 'internal major incident' in response to the pressure its accident and emergency department was under. In the week ending 4 January, just 80 per cent of the patients attending A&E had been seen, treated and admitted or discharged within four hours, well below the national target of 95 per cent. CUH cancelled the incident that afternoon and other hospitals around the country were declaring a 'major external incident', which is a level above what CUH had declared. Nevertheless, the fact that our hospital had to take this step was clearly a cause for concern – and also a political gift to Sarah.

MPs are jacks of all trades, not specialists. We have to know a little bit about everything because on any given day we might be helping a constituent access benefits to which they are entitled, raising a complaint with the chief executive of the local hospital or responding to correspondence about the current situation in northern Nigeria. When a story like this breaks, however, we have to develop a more detailed understanding of the issue very quickly. We can then respond to enquiries from constituents and the local media, identify whether there is anything we need to do to support our local hospital and rebut any political attacks.

In this case, CUH's A&E department wasn't alone in facing pressures. And reassuringly both the government and the hospital were giving me the same explanation as to what was causing the problem.

First, more people were visiting A&E (nationally, a million more people in 2014 than in 2010). Some of these people didn't need to go to there – in Croydon, there was evidence that some people, particularly in the north of the borough, were not registered with a GP and were therefore using A&E as their primary healthcare.

Second, with our population ageing and many elderly people living with chronic health conditions, an increasing proportion of those who were going to A&E required admission to hospital, particularly during the winter. The coalition government had provided a record £700 million to deal with these additional winter pressures, but clearly there were still problems.

Third, once these patients' conditions had been stabilised and they no longer required a bed in an acute hospital, it was taking too long to put the necessary arrangements in place to discharge them to a community hospital or residential home or arrange care to enable them to return home.

And finally, there were some specific problems locally. Under governments of both parties, the NHS in Croydon had never received its fair share of the national NHS budget. The coalition government had started to put this right, but there was still a long way to go. This meant that our hospital couldn't afford to employ as many staff as some other hospitals. And the A&E department itself needed modernising. It had been built in the 1980s to treat about 70,000 patients a year, but was currently treating around 120,000 patients.

On a political level, this story was clearly a gift to Labour, but they did have an Achilles heel. Thanks to devolution, the coalition government wasn't running the NHS throughout the UK. In Scotland, the SNP were in charge; in Northern Ireland, a cross-party coalition; and in Wales, Labour. In all three of these nations, A&E departments were performing less well than their counterparts in England.

Thankfully, the situation rapidly began to improve as a result of a relatively mild winter and some incredible work by the staff at CUH. In the week ending 18 January, 94 per cent of patients were seen, treated and admitted or discharged within four hours, only just below the target. We had avoided a serious A&E crisis, which would have had significant consequences for patients and, rather less importantly, for my campaign.

United in mourning

On 18 January came the sad news that Cllr Gerry Ryan had passed away after a long battle with cancer. He was just fifty-seven years old.

Gerry had been my Labour opponent at the 2010 general election and before that I had served with him as a councillor for a number of years. We got on well – he was the kind of person you could have a robust debate with in the council chamber and then a pint with afterwards. To me, he embodied everything that is best about the Labour movement. He was a proud trade unionist, who worked hard to secure better terms and conditions for those he represented. And he was Labour to his bones without being tribal – he would happily work with anyone to advance the things he believed in.

His funeral was a moving occasion, the church packed to the rafters. It was a reminder of the strength of the Labour movement, but also a moment of cross-party unity.

That unity could not last long, however. There was still a campaign to be fought.

Unemployment halved

The next week, I managed to get the focus back onto the economy.

The monthly employment statistics were published on 21 January. They showed that 1,473 of my constituents had claimed Jobseeker's Allowance (JSA) in December. That was 4 per cent (or 59 people) fewer than in November, 36 per cent (837 people) fewer than the same time the previous year and 50 per cent (1,470 people) fewer than when Labour left office in May 2010.

The news regarding youth unemployment was even better. Three hundred and sixty-five of the Croydon Central residents claiming JSA in December were between eighteen and twenty-four years old, down 28 per cent (140 people) from the previous year (although from November to December the number had remained static) and 53 per cent (405 people) fewer than when Labour left office.

And it wasn't just that unemployment was falling; it was falling quicker in Croydon Central than in most parts of the country. When Labour left office, unemployment in Croydon Central was higher than the national average. Now it was lower. In May 2010, 5.0 per cent of the working age population in Croydon Central were unemployed compared with 4.8 per cent nationally; now the figures were 2.5 per cent and 2.7 per cent respectively.

Each month when I tweeted the latest good news on jobs, various Labour activists would reply claiming that all these new jobs were part time and/or low paid. The statistics did not bear that out, though. Three quarters of the 1.75 million extra jobs that the British economy had created since May 2010 were full time and three quarters of the rise in employment has been in managerial, professional and associate professional jobs. There was absolutely no room for complacency – there were still far too many people out of work, in part-time work when they would like a full-time job or in a job that didn't pay well enough for them to make ends meet. These figures showed, however, that things were changing for the better.

Postergate

The argument about the unemployment figures was interrupted by a bit of drama caused by Croydon Council.

On 12 February, they started putting up posters around the town claiming that the coalition government was cutting their funding by £100 million over the next three years.

This immediately rang alarm bells. I didn't think the government had announced any figures for 2016/17 yet, let alone 2017/18. Once again, I started by going to the House of Commons Library to find out the facts. In this case, it was all very complicated, as the response below shows:

Dear Mr Barwell,

Below is a table with some of the key figures relating to Croydon Council.

The functions and responsibilities of councils change over time. Each year when the Department for Communities & Local Government (DCLG) announces the local government settlement it recalculates the previous year's figure as if all functions and responsibilities were the same. This is to provide a year-on-year percentage change. The actual local government settlement amount and the adjusted amount is shown in the first two columns below. The percentage change is the year-on-year change on the adjusted amount. On a like for like basis the government is cutting Croydon's settlement funding in 2015/16 by £21.3 million.

The DCLG do not recalculate further back than one year. This makes it very difficult to compare headline amounts from non-adjacent years. The National Audit Office has recently criticised the DCLG for not producing a time series set of figures to enable comparison over a period of time.

Croydon Council local government finance settlement, service expenditure and net revenue expenditure (£ millions)

	Formula grant/Settlement Funding Assessment			Total service expenditure	Specific and special grants	Net revenue expenditure
	Actual	Adjusted	% change			
2009/10		116.8				
2010/11	118.5	138.8	1.5%	577.4	294.2	259.6
2011/12	123.3	126.1	-11.2%	563.0	298.1	270.8
2012/13	116.0	166.8	-8.0%	546.9	301.4	264.5
2013/14	161.9	161.9	-2.9%	617.2	347.7	285.6
2014/15	146.4	149.4	-9.6%	615.2	347.1	277.5
2015/16	128.1		-14.2%			

Source: DCLG Local government finance settlements and local authority review expenditure and financing (various years)
Note: Year-on-year change is calculated on adjusted amount

The net revenue expenditure shown in the last column is the amount of Croydon's expenditure that is not covered by specific grants or income and therefore has to be covered by the local government finance settlement funding, council tax receipts and any use of reserves.

I hope this is of some use.

In essence, the coalition government was cutting Croydon's settlement funding by £21.3 million in 2015/16, but it hadn't yet announced figures for specific and special grants and it hadn't announced *any* figures for 2016/17 or 2017/18. And contrary to all the talk about cuts, Croydon Council's total service expenditure had increased under this government from £577 million in 2010/11 to £615 million in 2014/15 (although it had fallen if you allowed for inflation, but only by £7 million or 1 per cent).

© Tim Pollard

The Croydon Council poster that the Advertising Standards Agency ruled was designed to affect voters

Leaving aside the accuracy of the council's claims, local councils are supposed to deliver public services, not take part in political campaigns. What was Croydon Council doing funding these posters, particularly when it was claiming to be so short of money? My main concern was to get the posters taken down as soon as possible. I emailed everyone on my bulletin list, encouraging them to complain to Croydon Council's chief executive, Nathan Elvery. Judged by the number of responses that were copied to me, lots of people did so.

When I met Nathan to discuss the matter, he told me the council's view was that the posters were legal. Their purpose was to inform residents of the financial pressures that the council was facing, rather than to influence the election. However, in the light of my concerns he undertook to review the matter.

This was a reasonable response, but any attempt to claim the posters were not political was fatally compromised a few hours later by the leader of the council, Councillor Tony Newman. He told me on Twitter that the aim of the posters was to 'highlight government cuts to Croydon you voted for'. Whatever the merits of his argument – it was true that I had voted to reduce government funding for local councils, because I believed we needed to reduce government spending in order to eliminate the deficit – Tony had just admitted that the intention of the posters was to highlight my voting record. This was undeniably political and not something council taxpayers' money should have been spent on.

A few days later, the council quietly took down the posters. There was an amusing postscript to this story, however. We had written to the Advertising Standards Authority complaining that the posters were misleading. On 8 March, they finally replied, saying they couldn't rule on our complaint. It was beyond their remit, they said, because the clear intention of the poster was 'to affect voters taking part in the democratic process'.

When to let it go

When you're fighting an ultra-marginal seat, you're desperate for any local issue you can campaign on that differentiates you from your opponents. There is a danger, though. If you jump on every passing bandwagon, you begin to look like an opportunist who will say anything to get votes. This is the dilemma that confronted me over a proposed new secondary school at Croydon Sports Arena in the Woodside ward of my constituency.

Croydon has a rapidly growing school-age population so is desperately in need of additional school places. I had worked hard to get funding from the coalition government to help the council provide these places (between 2011 and 2015, we got seven times as much as in the previous four years).

There are two ways of providing new places: expanding existing schools and building new ones. Both are often unpopular because the people negatively affected – the parents of existing pupils at a school that is to be expanded (who might have chosen it because they thought their child would do better in a small school) or the people living close to the site of a proposed new school (who are often worried about the extra traffic from parents dropping off and picking up their children and, in the case of secondary schools, possible anti-social behaviour by pupils) – are generally quick to make their views known. On the other hand, those who would benefit from the proposal – the parents of children who might not otherwise get a school place in a few years' time – don't speak up because they don't yet know they are at risk of not getting a place.

The idea of a secondary school on this particular site had first arisen when the council was Conservative controlled. There was considerable local opposition based on concerns about possible anti-social behaviour by pupils, the impact on neighbouring

Metropolitan Open Land[18] and particularly traffic and parking (the area around the site consists of narrow roads that are already heavily parked).

When they were in opposition, the local Labour councillors had been very critical of the proposal. Now they were running the council they were supporting it, albeit having reduced the size of the school slightly. Residents came to me asking me to oppose it.

Politically, it was tempting. It was an issue that affected lots of people, most of them normally Labour supporters. However, I had supported the proposal in principle when the council was Conservative controlled. In addition, I'm a big supporter of Oasis, the chosen sponsor of the school. They'd done an amazing job turning round Ashburton High School, now Oasis Academy Shirley Park, which had recently been rated as outstanding in every regard by Ofsted. I therefore told residents that I couldn't object to the scheme in principle. I would, however, speak on their behalf at the Planning Committee meeting on 27 February that would determine the application to ask for a delay so that their concerns about traffic and parking could be addressed.

The council's own traffic assessment admitted that the area was going to be gridlocked during the morning rush hour, the afternoon school run and the evening rush hour. It also acknowledged that there weren't enough vacant spaces in the surrounding roads to cope with the number of parents expected to drive their children to and from school.

When I informed the council that I was intending to speak at the Planning Committee meeting, I was told that the Labour chairman of the committee, Paul Scott (who was a councillor for the area), had refused me permission to do so. He only backed down after an outcry from the local media and local residents, objecting to what appeared to be an effort to gag an elected representative.

---

18 Land within Greater London that has the same protection from development as the Green Belt.

At the meeting, I made it clear I accepted the need for a new school and was a big fan of Oasis. However, I asked the Planning Committee to insist on more parking on site, to rethink some of the proposed parking restrictions and to look at more radical measures to prevent the area from becoming gridlocked. Sadly, they wouldn't consider any of these suggestions and the application was approved as it was with all six Labour councillors, including two of the councillors for the area, voting in favour and the four Conservative councillors either voting against or abstaining.

Residents were furious with their local councillors and grateful to me for intervening, even if they wished I'd opposed the scheme in principle. I suspect the local councillors concerned learnt a lesson about not saying one thing when you're in opposition and then doing something else when you're in power.

Chapter 17

A rainforest of direct mail

In early March, we had a big decision to take about how to spend a large chunk of the money we had raised. The short campaign, with its very tight spending limits, was rapidly approaching. There was no slack in the budget for those final few weeks, but there was still plenty of room in our budget for the long campaign. The question was: how to use it?

It was no good printing any more leaflets. Our delivery network was at full stretch getting out those we had already produced. The choice was between advertising in our local papers and direct mail.

There was a heated debate among the campaign team. Advertising would allow us to reach more electors, but many of them would already have mind up their minds. The changes we had made to our canvassing technique meant we had the opportunity to do something more targeted – to focus on the voters who were going to determine the result of this election and to nuance our message depending on who we were writing to. What was the point of having spent hour after hour knocking on doors to identify specific types of floating voters if we weren't then going to do something with this data?

So in early March we unleashed a veritable rainforest of direct mail on the unsuspecting letterboxes of Croydon Central. Because volunteer time was at a premium and we had plenty of money, we paid for the mailings to be professionally produced.

Dave or Ed?

The first mailing was to undecided electors who preferred David Cameron to Ed Miliband as Prime Minister. The message was simple:

> This is the closest election in a generation; no one knows what the result is going to be ... But one thing's for certain – the only two people in with a chance of being Prime Minister are David Cameron and Ed Miliband. Who do you want representing Britain abroad for the next five years? Who do you trust to get the better deal for Britain in Europe? Who will stand up to the increasing threat posed by Russia? And who will make the right decisions to keep our economy growing and get us back into the black? If, like me, your answer to these questions is David Cameron then I hope you'll lend me your vote on 7 May.

The Barwell fan club

The second mailing was to undecided electors who wanted to keep me as their local MP. Again the message was simple:

> If you want me to continue doing this job, you need to vote for me on 7 May. In many parts of the country, the result is a foregone conclusion – the same party wins every time. But you live in one of the

closely fought constituencies that decide elections. Ladbrokes currently make my Labour opponent the 4/7 favourite to win this seat, with me at 5/4 and the other parties 100/1 outsiders. Your vote could make all the difference.

Squeezing the Labour vote

The third letter, to soft Labour voters, was more ambitious. Most of these people were going to vote Labour, but any we could attract would, to use a football analogy, be 'two-voters' – one off Labour's total as well as one onto ours.

I wrote about my passion to build a fairer society where kids from less well-off backgrounds get to go to a great school, there's full employment, people get a fair reward for a hard day's work, everyone pays their fair share in tax, people are judged by their actions not their skin colour or gender and people who work hard are better off than those who don't. We also used a quote from President Obama about the success of the coalition government's economic policies. I ended by acknowledging that the reader might not normally vote Conservative: 'You may normally support Labour, but if you're unsure about Ed Miliband and whether he can be trusted with our economy, I hope you feel that our politics are not so different and might consider lending me your vote this time.'

The BME vote

The fourth letter, which was to voters from black and ethnic minority communities, was equally ambitious. The letter focused on my opposition to UKIP and my record campaigning for reform of both stop-and-search and airline passenger duty; for action to tackle Islamophobia, the targeting of south Asian families by burglars and the persecution of Christians abroad; and for an independent investigation of alleged war crimes in Sri Lanka. Once again we used the quote from President Obama and once again I ended by acknowledging that the reader might not normally vote Conservative (though this time I hoped he or she may have conservative values):

> You may never have voted Conservative before, but if you share my values – the importance of family, the value of education, reward for hard work – and you think I have been a good MP, I hope you will lend me your vote on 7 May. At a time when UKIP are demonising immigrants and threatening to abolish the laws that prevent employers from racially discriminating, your vote could make all the difference.

Generation Y

The final letter was to first-time voters. This focused on our record on creating jobs, tackling abuse of stop-and-search and helping young first-time buyers as well as my opposition to UKIP and the fact that over 200 local young people had done work experience in my office. Once again, we used the quote from President Obama and I ended by appealing to the economic and social liberalism of Generation Y:

> If you share my belief in freedom to live the life we choose and keep more of the money we work hard to earn and you think I have been a good local MP, please give me your support on 7 May. This is going to be the closest election in a generation. At a time when UKIP are demonising immigrants and threatening to abolish the laws that prevent employers from racially discriminating, your vote could make all the difference.

You can see a copy of the last three letters on pages 254–9.

Who knows how well they worked? Political parties aren't large businesses that can afford to test such things. It was at least a big step forward from delivering the same leaflet through every door.

It was now just a few days until Parliament would be dissolved and I would finally be free to spend all my time on the campaign. I couldn't wait. I felt things were moving our way.

And then I was hit by the worst moment of the whole campaign.

Chapter 18

Embarrassment

PEOPLE ARE USED to politicians making claims about what a good job they've done. Quite rightly, they treat such self-promotion with a solid dose of scepticism. To counter that, a key element of our strategy was to get other people to endorse my work as a local MP. We'd secured a few high-profile endorsements for the campaign launch back in September. Now we set ourselves a much more ambitious target. We would try to recruit a couple of hundred local people who would be prepared to write a letter to their neighbours endorsing me.

The idea was that these letters should be personal – from people who knew me well or who I'd helped, explaining why they thought I was a good MP. We would print copies of each letter on plain paper in a handwriting font and deliver them in unstamped envelopes in the roads around where the letter writer lived. We believed that a recommendation from someone who lived nearby would be much more persuasive than me saying I was a good MP and that letters delivered in an unstamped envelope that appeared handwritten were much more likely to be read than yet another Conservative-branded leaflet.

This project was ambitious in several regards. First, it was going to be incredibly difficult to recruit that number of letter writers. People were likely to be understandably reticent about writing to their immediate neighbours about politics. Second, these letters would only be effective if they were personal. We couldn't draft them for people – they had to write them themselves. And third, even assuming we managed to recruit enough people and they all produced usable material, printing several hundred copies of each letter and getting them stuffed in addressed envelopes and then delivered, all in a short timescale, was going to be an enormous logistical challenge.

Given the very tight limits on how much you can spend during the short campaign, the letters would have to be printed in-house, which meant on our slightly tired office printer by Ian and Jason. They were already attending canvassing sessions, inputting canvassing data after those sessions, producing canvass cards and maps for the next session, managing the delivery network in half the constituency and probably doing lots of other things I wasn't even aware of. Nevertheless we were all agreed that the potential benefits justified the work involved so we decided to go ahead.

The first task was to recruit the letter writers. There were three distinct groups we approached: people who were active in the campaign and knew me well; personal friends; and people I had helped in some significant way during my five years as an MP.

In hindsight, we should have found the time to call on each of these people and speak to them in person, but time was short and we all had a million other things to do so I wrote the following letter:

Dear X,

I am writing to ask for a favour.

As you know, the forthcoming election here in Croydon Central is going to be very close – there's a real danger that my Labour opponent will win the seat. We are working very hard to try to stop that happening, knocking on people's doors to ask for their support and delivering a lot of literature setting out what I've done and what I'll do if I am re-elected for another five years.

But me telling people that I do a good job isn't that persuasive – I would say that, wouldn't I? Other people saying it is much more powerful. I'm therefore writing to ask if you would be prepared to write to people in your neighbourhood saying why you think I am a good local MP.

I know this is a lot to ask – most of us don't normally discuss politics with our neighbours! But I am not asking you to write a political letter – in fact, it'll be much more effective if it doesn't mention the Conservative Party or David Cameron. What I'm looking for is something personal that talks about how I've helped you or someone you know or an occasion when you met me. I've enclosed some letters that other people have written to give you a clearer idea.

Although it's a lot to ask, I hope you'll consider doing it. I think it could make a big difference to the result on 7 May. You wouldn't have to produce the letters – we'll take care of that. All you have to do is let us know what you'd like to say.

Yours sincerely,
Gavin Barwell MP

Normally when I write a leaflet or a piece of direct mail, I think very carefully about how my opponents could spin it when they inevitably see it. In this case, however, I was writing to a small group of people, all of whom were supporters, so I was careless. You can probably guess what happened next.

The people I wrote to may all have been Conservative supporters, but it turned out that the husband of one of them was not. He gave the letter to Labour, who in turn passed it on to Joe Murphy at the *Evening Standard* (I know who it was who leaked it to Labour, because although the *Standard* was careful to remove the name and address of the recipient, a Labour activist tweeted a photo of the full letter).

I duly got a call from Joe, who was interested in two angles. First, the phrase 'it'll be much more effective if it doesn't mention the Conservative Party or David Cameron' – was I trying to distance myself from the Prime Minister? And second, there were similarities between the letters we had attached – were they actually written by me or someone on the campaign and hence fake?

I explained that far from trying to distance myself from David Cameron, the choice between him and Ed Miliband was one of my key messages, repeated on nearly all of my literature. It was on the calling card we gave to every elector when we canvassed them or put through their door if they were not in. I had just signed off a large direct mail campaign to all the people we had canvassed as undecided but preferring David Cameron to Ed Miliband as Prime Minister. And I was using the CCHQ literature service for some of my leaflets, so they were bound to have David Cameron all over them. However, I added, there were some voters who didn't have a preference when it came to national politics, but who thought I was a good local MP. In an ultra-marginal seat I had to appeal to them too. That's where these endorsement letters came in.

On the issue of whether the letters were fake, there wasn't much I could say other than to reassure him that I would not be writing any of the letters. Not only would that be wrong, it would defeat the whole purpose of the exercise. The letters would only have a chance of changing people's voting intention if they were personal. I couldn't write them for people.

London Evening Standard

HARRY KANE IS THE ONLY MAN WHO CAN SAVE SPURS' SEASON

ADEBAYOR BANKS ON STRIKER TO RESCUE CHAMPIONS LEAGUE BID

LONDON TORY MP: DON'T MENTION CAMERON

... OR THE CONSERVATIVE PARTY BECAUSE IT WILL BE MORE EFFECTIVE, HE TELLS BACKERS

Conservative Party or David Cameron," he wrote. Labour said it showed that he regarded the Tory leader as a liability. One Labour MP compared his letter with John Cleese's comic hotelier Basil Fawlty telling staff "don't mention the war" in front of German guests, in ... offended.

This *Evening Standard* front page was, for me, the worst moment of the campaign

Joe was clearly going to run the story, but having given him all the facts I hoped it wouldn't be too prominent. The next day, Monday 16 March, I was on the front page of the *Evening Standard*.

For me, this was the worst moment of the whole campaign. I felt like I'd let the party down. I was furious with myself for not being more careful about the phrasing of the letter. I wrote to the Prime Minister to apologise and included a quote from my calling card about the choice between him and Ed Miliband for use if any Labour MPs raised the story during PMQs. I got a nice message back via his parliamentary private secretary, but it didn't make me feel much better.

If I was furious with myself, I was also cross with the *Standard*.

I understood that the 'It'll be much more effective if it doesn't mention the Conservative Party or David Cameron' quote made for an easy headline, but beneath that there was really no story here. Far from distancing myself from David Cameron, I was trying to make my campaign about the choice of him or Ed Miliband as Prime Minister. And as time would tell, the letters weren't fake. You can judge for yourself – I've included an example on page 265.

Being on the front page of the *Standard* made us much more nervous about approaching people to write these letters. As a result, we ended up producing fewer than fifty of them, which meant we didn't have a letter writer for some areas and some people therefore got a letter from someone who lived a few roads away rather than in their road or a neighbouring one.

When we got around to delivering the letters in late April, however, our decision to proceed was vindicated. The response from voters was very positive. Reading them again now, some of the letters are very moving. Despite the painful headline, if I could go back and run the whole campaign again I'd put even more effort into recruiting letter writers. I'd just be much more careful about how I went about it.

That learning was in the future, though. When I went home on the day the *Standard* ran the story, I was feeling pretty low.

Fortunately, better news was on its way.

Chapter 19

Final days at Westminster

A little encouragement

THE NEXT DAY, Michael Ashcroft published the results of his second poll of Croydon Central. It wasn't good news – we were still behind – but we were catching up.

On the first voting intention question – 'If there was a general election tomorrow, which party would you vote for?' – Labour had increased their lead:

Labour	41 per cent (+5)
Conservatives	33 per cent (+2)
UKIP	16 per cent (-7)
Greens	6 per cent (+2)
Liberal Democrats	3 per cent (-1)

(The figures in brackets show the change from the November 2014 poll.)

On the second voting intention question, however – 'Thinking specifically about your own parliamentary constituency at the next general election and the candidates who are likely to stand for election to Westminster there, which party's candidate do you think you will vote for in your own constituency?' – which was generally accepted as the better indicator of the likely result on 7 May, the news was better. Both main parties had increased their share of the vote compared with the previous poll, but I was closing the gap:

Labour	41 per cent (+2)
Conservatives	37 per cent (+4)
UKIP	13 per cent (-6)
Greens	5 per cent (+2)
Liberal Democrats	3 per cent (-1)

And this time there was evidence that I had a personal vote. Michael Ashcroft observed: 'Croydon Central ... shows the biggest shift [of all the seats polled in this batch] between the standard voting intention question and the result when people are asked to think about their own constituency and the candidates likely to stand there.'

The number of people saying that they would definitely not vote Labour was unchanged at 39 per cent; the number saying they would definitely not vote Conservative was down 2 percentage points at 46 per cent. There had also been little change to the answers people gave when they were asked what kind of government they wanted to see after 7 May 2015:

A Labour government	35 per cent (+1)
A Conservative government	28 per cent (+1)
A coalition between Labour and the Liberal Democrats	12 per cent (+1)
A coalition between the Conservatives and the Liberal Democrats	11 per cent (+2)

Ed Miliband had improved his ratings slightly, but was still miles behind. Thirty-one per cent (+1) were satisfied with the job David Cameron was doing overall as Prime Minister, 32 per cent (+5) were dissatisfied and would prefer to have Ed Miliband as Prime Minister instead and 23 per cent (-4) were dissatisfied with David Cameron and yet would still prefer to have him as PM than Ed Miliband.

Economic optimism had increased even further. Sixty-four per cent now thought the economy would fare well over the next year for them and their family, compared with 32 per cent who thought it would fare badly.

Once again, there was some useful intelligence in the underlying data. More people who had voted Conservative in 2010 were now planning to do so again (71 per cent, up 4 percentage points). Fewer were planning to switch to UKIP (15 per cent, down 8 points). And we were now doing much better among 2010 Liberal Democrats – 31 per cent were planning to vote for me (20 points more than in November 2014) compared with 33 per cent who were planning to vote Labour (12 points lower than in November 2014).

Finally, with just seven weeks to go we were still matching Labour on local activity. Forty-five per cent of those polled had been contacted over the last few weeks by us and 45 per cent by Labour.

This poll was great for morale. It suggested our strategy – to make the election about keeping David Cameron as Prime Minister and me as the local MP and to focus on the economy – was right. It also showed we were matching Labour on the ground. And it indicated that what we were doing was working.

We still weren't winning, though. We were 4 points behind and we had less than two months to change that. I felt like an athlete in a long-distance race chasing down someone who has broken free from the pack. I was reeling Sarah in, but did I have enough time left to overtake her on the home straight?

The Chancellor lends a helping hand

There were lots of things that I disagreed with the Labour council about, but on the most important issue – the regeneration of our town centre – we were in complete agreement.

The Labour administration had continued the policies they had inherited from the previous Conservative administration – the redevelopment of the Whitgift Centre by Westfield and Hammerson, the investment in improving public spaces in the town centre, the modernisation of the Fairfield Halls and the various masterplans the council had agreed with the major landowners in the town centre. And to their credit, they had done a good job of bringing all this together to show how the regeneration of Croydon town centre could be of a similar scale to the planned new garden city at Ebbsfleet, but achievable in half the time.

This regeneration won't happen, however, without improvements to the town's infrastructure, in particular its roads, public transport and power network. And there was a gap between the resources that the council had available to make the required improvements (including projected contributions from the various developers) and what was needed. The council therefore asked Labour's Steve Reed, the Croydon North MP, and me to work with them to lobby the coalition government for help to close this gap. They christened the idea 'Croydon Growth Zone'.

The case was simple. If the government helped Croydon Council to close the gap – perhaps by letting the council keep the extra tax generated by the first phase of regeneration – the council would use this money to fund further phases. The government would lose a little tax income, but thousands of jobs would be created and thousands of new homes built.

The Chancellor signalled his support for the idea in his Budget on 18 March and announced some initial funding. He was also very clear about who had convinced him: 'London is the global capital of the world and we want it to grow stronger still. That is why we are investing in the Croydon Growth Zone, proposed and championed by Gavin Barwell.'

Speak to any Conservative MP who was defending a marginal seat at the last election and they will tell you the same thing: there was no member of the government who did more to help those of us who were on the frontline.

A new A&E department for Croydon

Government support for the Croydon Growth Zone was important for the long-term future of the town and helpful politically, but at that moment it was an abstract concept. There was one more announcement I needed before Parliament dissolved and the final phase of the campaign began, something much more tangible.

In 2008, the Care Quality Commission had said that the accident and emergency department at Croydon University Hospital (CUH) was badly designed, in a poor state of repair and too small to cope with the number of patients it was treating. The trust that was responsible for running the hospital had developed a plan for a new A&E, which would be a third bigger than the current department and have an open-plan design, giving clinicians clear sight of their patients to improve safety and care, as well as doors rather than curtains on all 'majors' cubicles to improve patient privacy and dignity.

I had been lobbying in support of this bid for some time. By mid-March, I knew it had been approved, but there was a frustrating delay in announcing the news. Finally on 26 March, the day Parliament was dissolved, the NHS Trust Development Authority announced that CUH would receive £21.25 million. Work could get underway almost immediately.

This was great news for Croydon and a testament to everyone who had worked so hard to put together the bid. It was also great news for me. It was an example of how a good MP can make a difference, securing funding from the government to change their constituency for the better. And it was also proof of the Conservative Party's commitment to the NHS in Croydon and therefore a formidable shield against Labour's main message – the claim that Conservatives don't care about our health service.

We produced a leaflet, which we distributed to every home in the constituency over the next few days (see page 264). Jeremy Hunt visited the hospital to meet the staff in A&E and issued a press release saying:

> It's fantastic news that the plan for an investment of over £21 million in a new emergency department at Croydon hospital can now go ahead. Gavin Barwell has been a strong local advocate for this project – one that will bring highly advanced new urgent and emergency care capacity for the people of Croydon and allow the hospital to provide the best possible care.

In my press release, I focused on those who deserved most credit – the staff at CUH who had put together a great bid – as well as my personal commitment to our NHS:

> I want to thank John Goulston, chief executive of Croydon Health Services Trust, Dr Kathryn Channing, lead clinician for Emergency Medicine at Croydon University Hospital, and their team for producing such a great bid and the government for giving us the investment our hospital needs and deserves.
>
> I am very passionate about our NHS. My wife works for it as a speech and language therapist, it saved my life when I had cancer as a child and it gave outstanding care to my dad when he was dying of Alzheimer's – my family will be forever grateful for the support the NHS provided to us as he was taken away from us day by day.

> Since I was elected as an MP, I have tried to pay back the debt I owe, supporting increases in the NHS budget, getting the formula the government uses to distribute the NHS budget around the country changed so that Croydon gets a fairer deal and now securing funding for a new emergency department.
>
> The NHS isn't perfect, but the principle – that if you get sick or hurt you don't have to worry whether you can afford treatment – is one of the best things about this country and I will continue to do everything I can to defend and improve it.

After issuing this release, I cleared my desk in the whips' office and left Westminster, possibly for the last time. If I wasn't coming back, at least my last act as an MP was to secure something that was going to benefit thousands of people in my home town.

Chapter 20

Hustings

MY STRATEGY THROUGHOUT the campaign was not to respond to anything Sarah Jones said unless she came up with a very good idea (in which case I would quickly get behind it) or made a serious mistake. If I got drawn into responding to whatever she was saying it would simply make it a bigger story, helping her to build name recognition. I was better focusing on communicating my own message.

Towards the end of an election campaign, however, various organisations hold hustings. These are meetings where the candidates are invited to appear on the same stage to answer questions from members of the public (sometimes all the candidates are invited, sometimes just those from the major parties). Obviously, in situations like these I couldn't avoid responding to Sarah. The question, therefore, was how many of them to do.

Most MPs try to do as few as possible. As the incumbents, they're generally keen to avoid a format that places them on the same footing as all the other candidates. They have more to lose and less to gain. Because they've been doing the job, they're expected to have more detailed knowledge of both local issues and national policy and therefore to perform better. If the incumbent wins the debate, it's not really news. If they get beaten by their main opponent, it's a big story. So why take the risk?

I took a different view. I believed that as a format hustings played to my strengths. Not only did I have a better knowledge of the detail having been the MP for five years, I had got into politics through debating – plus, my centrist views would make me a difficult target to attack. I also believed that hustings would not play to Sarah's strengths. She is highly personable and speaks well, but from what I had seen so far I felt she was less good at answering difficult questions, something journalists on both the local papers had said to me privately as well. I therefore thought I would do well in any head-to-head.

There was another advantage that I hoped I would gain. If, as I suspected, Sarah shared my assessment of how we would do in a head-to-head, she would spend much more time than me preparing for the meetings. That would mean she had less time to spend out knocking on doors. I suspected she would come across well on the doorstep, so the less time she was able to spend there, the happier I was.

I therefore set about encouraging as many organisations as possible to hold hustings.

Trial run

The Croydon Area Gay Society organised the first hustings on 18 November, nearly six months before polling day. This was a useful trial run and it confirmed all my suspicions.

Sarah's opening speech was very good. It focused on how she had got involved in politics after listening to a speech the then Conservative Cabinet minister Peter Lilley gave back in the mid-1990s, which she felt was an attack on teenage mums like her – and how, as a result, she would always stand up for minorities. Things were different, though, when we got into detailed exchanges. On three issues – the dodgy figures Labour HQ had given her regarding long-term unemployment in Croydon Central, the mess the council had got into on school playing fields and the council's policy of reducing the proportion of homes available for ownership – she really struggled under detailed questioning.

It was evidence of how hard it is to stand against a sitting MP. These were all issues that I was dealing with day in, day out. Sarah, on the other hand, had to get up to speed on all these issues while holding down a completely separate day job. It's called incumbency advantage for a reason.

Several members of my campaign team had come along to take detailed notes. They went away confident that our decision to encourage lots of hustings meetings was going to pay off. Their one piece of advice was to make sure I got the tone right when questioning what Sarah had said. If I was too aggressive, I could win the argument but leave the audience sympathising with Sarah.

Twelve hustings in twenty days

The next hustings meeting was nearly five months later, on 10 April. It was organised by Croydon Business Improvement District. The audience was mainly businesspeople from the town centre plus a few members of the rival campaign teams.

It was just Sarah and me on the platform, my preferred format. I offered her the chance to speak first, suspecting she would use the same speech as in November. When she duly did, I was able to rebut some of her points in my opening speech. In the question-and-answer session that followed, I was able to use my greater knowledge of the detail of what was going on in the town to good effect as well as catch her out on Labour's policy on corporation tax (she boasted about Labour's record of keeping corporation tax low without mentioning that their manifesto included a commitment to increase it).

The most interesting exchange, however, was in response to a question about the possibility of a Labour–SNP deal if there was a hung parliament. Sarah was clearly very uncomfortable about defending this, but she was also unwilling to say that she wouldn't support it. I'm guessing she thought it was a real possibility and so didn't want to box herself in, but hedging bets is rarely a good look for a politician. We hadn't planted this question – it had come up spontaneously, which was an indication that more and more people were concerned about the issue.

The feedback from members of the audience after the meeting was very positive. It had gone even better than the trial run back in November.

Over the next nineteen days, there were a further eleven hustings so we all became fairly familiar with the key arguments. The next two were both on the evening of 14 April at two local schools, Cambridge Tutors College and Coloma Convent Girls' School. The possibility of a Labour–SNP deal was raised at both of these meetings as well. Sarah had clearly given some thought to how to handle this. Rather than answer the question, she challenged me to rule out working with UKIP. This might have been a tricky question for some Conservatives, but it was a gift for me. Whatever position the Conservative Party nationally took, there was no way I would work with someone like Nigel Farage, who I felt was pandering to racism. I was very happy to say so in unambiguous terms. In return, would she rule out supporting a Labour–SNP deal? No, she wouldn't.

At the next meeting, on the Monks Hill estate on 15 April, Sarah fell into the 'promising more than you can deliver' trap.

The council was in dispute with a local school about who should manage a new community centre that was on the school site. As a result, a local over-50s group was unable to access the centre. Sarah announced at the hustings meeting that they would have access by 25 April. That got her through the meeting, but it cost her votes when she subsequently wasn't able to get the council to deliver on her promise.

The next night Sarah and I attended a hustings organised by Croydon Citizens, a collection of faith, education and civic institutions. Looking back, I feel this was my best performance of any of the meetings. The audience was not naturally Conservative and the format was very different: rather than ask us standard questions about each party's policies, they wanted our support for four campaigns they were running on youth employability, a living wage for people working in social care, indefinite detention of migrants and refugees, and affordable housing. Instead of trying to score political points, I tried to change their perceptions of the Conservative Party and explain why I believed their progressive aims on reducing youth unemployment, increasing pay and helping people own their own homes were more likely to be achieved by Conservative policies. And rather than tell them exactly what they wanted to hear on indefinite detention, I gave an honest answer, saying I shared their concern but also trying to explain the difficulties the government faced. I got some lovely feedback at the end of the evening.

Further hustings organised by our local branch of the Federation of Small Businesses and Archbishop Tenison's Church of England High School followed, before the one occasion our strategy came unstuck.

I had agreed to attend a hustings organised by the National Union of Teachers on 21 April. I knew before I turned up that I was in for a rough ride. First, many in the teaching profession opposed large elements of the coalition government's education reforms. And second, the panel would consist of me; Sarah; Christine Blower, the general secretary of the NUT; and an ex-headmaster, who I was pretty confident would not be a Conservative supporter. I would probably be outnumbered three to one.

On the night, there was a banner in the room which read, 'Croydon NUT: Solidarity Forever'. I didn't feel much solidarity. The banner pretty much summed up the meeting, though: an understandable focus on the welfare of teachers, but very little talk of raising educational standards. At every turn, Sarah told the NUT members what they wanted to hear, even opposing key reforms that the Blair government had introduced.

The moment that really angered me, though, was when we got onto selective education. I argued that we shouldn't go back to the days when all children had to sit an exam in their final year at primary school that decided whether they went to a grammar or secondary modern, but that I'd like to see a couple of selective schools in Croydon. Quite a lot of Croydon parents sit their children for grammar schools in neighbouring Bromley and Sutton, so there's clearly demand for this type of education (in the interests of transparency, I'm one of those parents – my eldest goes to Wallington County Grammar School).

To my amazement, Sarah disagreed. I understand that some people are opposed to selective education on principle and respect their point of view, but Sarah had paid to send her own children to selective private schools. To then oppose bright kids from less privileged backgrounds being able to go to a selective school was a pretty blatant example of the 'do as we say, not as we do' approach of some on the left. I was sorely tempted to make the audience aware that she had sent her children to private schools. This was one of those moments, however, where the fact that I knew Sarah and worked with her mum on the board of a local charity led me to behave differently than I would otherwise have done. I didn't want to drag her family into it so I kept quiet.

At the end of the meeting, we were asked what we would do if we lost the election. I said I didn't know, but had thought about teaching. Sarah couldn't resist a quip that I needed to get my teaching qualifications before I was allowed in front of a class,[19] which the audience loved. Game, set, match.

I went home very angry – at the NUT for having a panel I felt was far from balanced and at myself, both for being too soft with Sarah and for agreeing to participate in the first place. When I got home, however, I got an email from a parent, who had sat at the back of the room. They said they had been appalled at the attitudes of some in the audience, but too scared to say anything. They ended the email by saying that if I did lose, they would be very happy for me to teach their child whether or not I was formally qualified. It had been worth my while going after all.

Two days later, we had a hustings at Quest Academy. This was probably the most fun of all of them. There were several hundred pupils there and they really enjoyed us having a robust debate. Most of the young people were from black and minority ethnic backgrounds and they gave Peter Staveley, the UKIP candidate, a pretty hard time. Later that evening, we had another hustings, this one organised by South Croydon Community Association. This was a bit of a non-event, because they invited all seven candidates, rather than just the five main parties. There is clearly a democratic argument for doing this, but on the other hand giving someone who ended up getting fifty-seven votes the same airtime as the candidates for the major parties is a bit strange and limits the debate.

We were in the home stretch now. The *Croydon Advertiser* hustings on 27 April and Cedars School hustings on 29 April both went off fairly well. Now there was only one to go.

---

19 Labour's manifesto included a commitment to require all teachers to be formally qualified. The Conservative Party's position was that this should be the norm, but that some people who didn't have a formal teaching qualification nonetheless made outstanding teachers, so it should be up to headmasters to decide who should be allowed to teach in their schools.

The final showdown

On 2 May, the *Croydon Citizen*, a non-profit community newspaper, held the final hustings of the campaign. It was chaired by Tom Black, a Labour activist. I knew him well and had no doubt that he would be scrupulously fair.

He didn't have an easy job. This was the only hustings meeting where both parties had a fair few activists in the audience and there was some fairly aggressive barracking from both sides. Having been an MP for five years, I was used to dealing with this; Sarah was not.

From the outset, she was much more aggressive than she had been in the previous meetings. I suspected the final Ashcroft poll, which had been published the day before and showed me ahead by 4 percentage points (see Chapter 21), had spooked her campaign team and she had been told to get personal. I wasn't sure if this new, more aggressive style would suit her because she's not that kind of person, and so it proved.

The first question was, 'What are the best qualities of your opponent?' I had no difficulty saying something positive about her: 'I would say Sarah's best quality is her passion. Being with her in all these hustings meetings and having known her for a while ... I think she has a genuine passion for what she believes in.'

She, on the other hand, found it impossible to be wholly positive:

> Um... It's a tricky question. I think that probably I'd accept that Gavin is a hard-working MP. I think he says that very often on lots of his literature. I think for me that's the starting point of what you should expect an MP to be. Of course an MP should be hard-working, but he should be so much more and where I disagree so fundamentally with Gavin is the policies that he votes on in Parliament. He voted against an £8 minimum wage and for a tax cut for millionaires.

We moved onto the economy. Someone asked Sarah the hundred-million-dollar question: did she think the last Labour government had spent too much money? Ed Miliband had been asked this a few days before on TV when he was being interviewed by members of a studio audience and had said, 'No.' The audience reaction – a mixture of astonishment and derision – had been one of the defining moments of the campaign. Sarah gave the same answer and got the same reaction. Someone else asked her about the last Labour government selling off our gold reserves at the bottom of the market, to which she gave this laugh-out-loud response: 'It was sold at the price that it was at at the time. [Laughter] At the time, it was sold at a good price.'

We then moved onto the NHS and had a revealing exchange on whether we should judge how well it was doing by considering individual case studies or aggregate data:

SJ: The eighteen-week wait from referral to treatment, they are not meeting that target—

GB: But it's better than it was under Labour. Eighteen weeks is lower than it was under Labour.

SJ: You can't say that, no.

GB: Yes it is. There's fewer people waiting eighteen weeks, there's fewer people waiting twenty-six weeks—

SJ: This is just schoolboy debating!

GB: It's not 'schoolboy', they're facts.

SJ: Look at the NHS, ask your constituents. I met a man the other day who came into my office the day after his wife had died. He had called an ambulance, who said, 'You are not a priority, call us back in twenty minutes.' He called again in twenty minutes' time, his wife was in agony. They said, 'Come back again, call us back in twenty minutes.' He called again, he called again, the ambulance finally arrived an hour and a half later and his wife died. We are facing real problems in the health service and you must see that in the people that you talk to in Croydon. This back and forth with the stats, you know, it's very clever politics but the reality is there for people in Croydon to see.

GB: Here again you see a real distinction between us because when Sarah is pressed in an argument she relies upon an individual story. Of course there are people that don't get a good experience from the NHS, I see that as the MP and I help them take it up with the NHS. But there are such things as facts. You just said the number of people waiting eighteen weeks has not declined under this government. It has. Fewer people are waiting eighteen weeks, fewer people are waiting twenty-six weeks, fewer people are waiting fifty-two weeks... the performance is better than under the Labour government. You can't deny that. The number of patients facing the indignity of mixed-sex wards was 12,000, nearly, when you left office – it was 225 in February this year. Hospital infections have virtually halved. So everyone should be clear what the facts are. Yes, the NHS isn't perfect; yes, there are still people that get a bad experience; but the independent data shows more people are satisfied with the NHS today than they were when Labour were in office and on virtually every measure the NHS is performing better today than it was in 2010.

Next was a question about Virgin Care running the urgent care centre at our local hospital. We both agreed that it didn't make sense to have one organisation running the urgent care centre and a different organisation running the emergency department with which it was co-located. Once again, however, Sarah's lack of knowledge of the detail let her down and I had a stroke of luck that someone who worked for the NHS was in the audience and backed me up when I corrected her:

SJ: Basically Virgin take the slightly easier cases and the A&E

doctors take the harder cases, so what it means is that if you're a doctor, you're looking to go into A&E and you want to work in London, you're not going to want to work in Croydon.

GB: You said that Virgin are just cherry-picking the easy cases. That is how an urgent care centre works. You have urgent care centres all around the country – the doctor over there is nodding – urgent care centres take less emergency cases. When a patient comes in and they've got a critical issue they go straight into the emergency department. The urgent care centre deals with things like when I took my son there because he'd cut his toe ... So it's not Virgin cherry-picking the patients—

SJ: It's a different system to the other hospitals. I've talked to these doctors—

GB: No, it's not a different system. It's not a different system. It is quite scary that someone standing for public election can so misunderstand how the health service works. [*Applause*] Just watch the member of NHS staff at the back of the room who was nodding when I spoke.

By this point, I think Sarah knew she was struggling. She sought to explain to the audience why: 'We're two very different people. Gavin went to Cambridge, president of the Union, went to work in Tory Central Office and became an MP. He's good at this sixth-form debating.'

This was a bizarre line of attack, as I explained:

Debating is part of the job, in the House of Commons that's what we do. But... Sarah is trying to pretend that we're very different people. I went to an independent school, I went to a Russell Group university and then I went to work in politics after university, she's quite right. Sarah went to an independent school, a Russell Group university, then went to work for a Member of Parliament, so we're not quite as different as she tries to make out.

A different Labour candidate could have attacked my background, but to this day I cannot believe that Sarah tried it. She knew that I was aware of her background and was bound to point it out. I can only presume that she had been told to attack and, in the heat of the moment, saw an opportunity and went for it without thinking it through.

After two hours, the debate drew to a close. We were each asked to give a final two-minute statement. Sarah went first and used her time to attack me, which went down pretty badly with the audience:

> Next week you face a choice. Do you want an MP who says one thing here in Croydon and then does another when he goes into Parliament, [*heckling*] who says he supports the minimum wage but voted against an £8 minimum wage in Parliament, who voted for a tax break for millionaires, who voted to scrap the general equality duty,[20] who voted for the bedroom tax, who says he's a strong voice in Parliament on all his leaflets but hasn't spoken for two years? [*Shouts of 'He's a whip!'*]

I sat there listening, trying to decide whether to rebut what she had said or stick to what I had planned to say. Other than a passing reference, I decided to ignore it:

> I've got some positive things to say. There's so many things that could decide how you're going to vote on 7 May, but I would argue to you that there is one thing that is more important than anything else and that's the economy. Because when the economy does well we should all benefit and when the economy does well our government should get more tax income for our NHS, for our schools, for all the things that really matter in life. Things are not perfect in

---

20 A duty on public authorities to consider how their decisions affect people who are protected under the Equality Act 2010. The coalition government had considered scrapping this duty – hence Sarah's reference – but had subsequently decided to keep it.

> Croydon today, they're not perfect in the country as a whole, but it is undeniable that they are in a better place than they were five years ago. The economy is growing more strongly than any other major economy in the world. Unemployment here in Croydon Central has been halved. The deficit has been more than halved. Inflation is low. Wages and living standards are now rising.
>
> So the question you have to ask yourself is: is this the point to make a change? Is this the point to change the people in charge? I would argue to you that it's not ...
>
> It has been a huge honour to be your MP for the last five years ... Sarah may believe that I don't speak up for Croydon. I think most of the people that live in my seat, whatever their politics, think I do do that. I'm very passionate about this town ... Thank you for coming tonight and I hope you'll give me your support on 7 May.

I felt it was clear I had got the better of the debate. Even some of Sarah's supporters came up and congratulated me afterwards. Best of all, though, my two oldest boys, who'd come to see what their dad had been up to for the last year, were seriously impressed. And they're *never* impressed by me ('embarrassing' and 'unfair' would be their most common adjectives).

If a reasonable proportion of swing voters had seen the debate, it might have changed lots of minds, but constituency hustings aren't shown on TV like the debates between the party leaders. There were about 100 people in the room, most of whom had already made up their minds. My performance would make next to no difference to the outcome of the election.

But it did feel good.

Chapter 21

The end is nigh

Conservative Campaign Headquarters to the rescue

SHORTLY BEFORE THE short campaign got underway, we were added to the Conservative Party's target seat list. This was a welcome recognition of the pressure we were under and it had four immediate benefits.

First, electors in Croydon Central started to receive national direct mail. This wasn't easy for CCHQ to do thanks to our decision not to use their canvassing script and to misuse some of the standard voting intention codes.[21] Nevertheless they found a way to do it, while gently suggesting that in future we might like to do as we were told.

---

21 If they wanted to mail a particular type of voter across all their target seats – people who were undecided between us and UKIP, say – they would have to do a different data selection for Croydon Central because we were recording voting intention information in a different way (see Chapter 6).

Second, we were now eligible for ministerial visits. The purpose of a ministerial visit is to secure media coverage. Because our local newspapers were only published once a week, there wasn't much point in having more than one major visit a week – you'd only get one story, no matter how many ministers turned up. However, every minister was under orders to spend a certain number of days visiting target seats. It was obviously easier to visit Croydon Central than a target seat in Cornwall or Cumbria, so we were inundated with people wanting to come. If more than one minister wanted to come in a given week, we suggested that the most helpful thing the second minister could do was to join us for a canvassing session. If I emailed all my potential activists to say that a minister was joining us, it would double or in some cases treble the turnout at that session.

It was interesting to see how different ministers responded to this. Some declined to come if they weren't going to get any media coverage. Others were complete stars, most notably Greg Clark, Michael Gove, Theresa May and Tina Stowell. One of the more surreal moments of the campaign was watching Theresa canvassing accompanied by a protection officer, who would stand a discreet distance away admiring the elector's front garden, and her bulletproof car, which kept pace with her along the road.

The third benefit was that we started to get more outside help. We were already getting huge amounts from Croydon South and some from the three Bromley seats and East Surrey, but they were now joined by three of my closest friends from the whips' office: Anne Milton, David Evennett and Damian Hinds. I don't know if the three of them have any idea how much of a difference it made having at least one of them with me most days.

When a Cabinet minister visits it's quite stressful. You want the visit to go well so the minister leaves with a good impression of your campaign. You also don't want to depress them, so you try to be as upbeat as possible. However, Anne, David and Damian were close friends. I didn't have to worry about impressing them (it was too late for that), I could be honest with them about how I was feeling and it was great to have people who weren't intimately involved with the campaign but knew a lot about campaigning who I could bounce ideas off. Plus we worked them hard too, of course.

Stephen Greenhalgh and Kit Malthouse, two of Boris Johnson's deputies, were also regular visitors, as was Mark Hoban. Mark was standing down as the MP for Fareham at this election, so he was under no obligation to come and help. He had been a highly competent minister in both the Treasury and the Department for Work and Pensions, but I now discovered that he is also an outstanding doorstep canvasser.

The final benefit was that the CCHQ call centre started calling Croydon Central electors to supplement our door-to-door canvassing. In principle this was great, but we didn't want inexperienced canvassers calling people we had placed in specific target voter groups and overwriting this information, so we asked them to focus solely on calling uncanvassed electors.

There's no doubt in my mind that the help we received from CCHQ in those last few weeks made the difference between winning and losing.

SNP *double whammy?*

As we approached the short campaign, the party's national message changed slightly. It was becoming clearer by the day that the SNP were going to gain lots of Labour seats in Scotland.[22] This meant there was no chance of Labour winning an overall majority and that subtly changed the choice at the election. It was now between David Cameron carrying on as Prime Minister or Ed Miliband, supported by Alex Salmond.

---

22 In the event, they won all but one of them.

CCHQ had picked up from their research that framing the choice in this way increased electors' concerns about Ed Miliband becoming Prime Minister. They were already expressing real doubts about whether he was up to the job. Now there was the added worry of whether he would be influenced by the SNP and what that could mean in terms of dealing with our debts, retaining our nuclear deterrent, funding for Scotland and most importantly the future of our Union.[23]

Even before we started using this message, electors were raising it with us spontaneously. When that happens, you know you're on to something.

A day in the life of a marginal seat candidate

Now that Parliament had been dissolved, I was free to devote myself to the campaign full time. I'd get up each morning at 5.30 and reply to emails or draft the next leaflet. The core campaign team of Ian, Jason, Sara, Mario, Katrina, Tim and myself would meet at 9 a.m. every other day at my house. The first canvassing session was at 11 a.m. followed by a quick pub lunch, where Jason would continue his quest to break the world record for eating a burger and chips.[24] After lunch, there would be another canvassing session. I tried to have an hour and a half with my family from 4.15 to 5.45 p.m., although some of that time was invariably taken up by calls that needed to be made. Then it was back out canvassing at 6 p.m. followed by a house meeting or hustings and then a couple of hours clearing emails.

It was a gruelling schedule – the only quality time off was on Sunday mornings, when we didn't have a canvass session. It was

23 The SNP favoured even higher borrowing than Labour, they wanted to get rid of our nuclear deterrent, they would understandably push for the best possible deal for Scotland and their objective was obviously to secure Scottish independence from the UK.

24 Provided said burger was not accompanied by anything green.

only for six weeks, though. I'd have a chance to rest after the election. If I won, there'd be a break while a new coalition agreement was hammered out.[25] And if I lost, well, I'd have plenty of spare time on my hands.

As I drove around the constituency, I kept playing the song 'Waves' by Mr Probz. It starts with the lines: 'My face above the water / My feet can't touch the ground.' It pretty much summed up how I felt.

People like you are backing Gavin Barwell

Our first leaflet of the short campaign was dedicated solely to endorsements (see pages 262–3). We worked hard to get a good mix of people in terms of age and ethnicity as well as people from each of the places that make up the constituency. The people who had voted for Andrew Pelling in 2010 were clearly going to be crucial, so we included an endorsement from a prominent local activist Shirley Trimmer, who had been one of his strongest supporters.

Ashburton ward, which we had lost in the council elections the year before, would be crucial too, so we also included an endorsement from Eddy Arram, a popular former councillor for that ward. We also included a QR code on the leaflet so people could use their smartphones to take them to a website where they could watch videos of the endorsements, rather than just reading the short quotes we were able to include in the leaflet (if you're interested, you can view any of the videos at www.gavinbarwell.com/videos).

Of all the pieces of literature we distributed in the ten months leading up to polling day, this was one of only four that electors mentioned unprompted on the doorstep.

---

25 Given the polls, another hung parliament looked inevitable.

Boris mania

On 9 April, we had the first of what would be three visits from the Mayor of London during the short campaign.

A Boris visit is unlike any other political visit. In terms of the reaction he gets from the public, he's more of a celebrity than a politician. This imposes a constraint: you can't walk very far because wherever you go you will be mobbed by people wanting selfies with him. On the other hand, he doesn't have the same level of security as a senior Cabinet minister and he's up for almost anything, so there's more opportunity to adapt the programme as you go than there would be for a visit by the Prime Minister or the Chancellor.

On this occasion, we decided to take him to Lower Addiscombe Road, one of the district centres in my constituency. It didn't have anything like the footfall you would get in Croydon town centre,

After a morning campaigning, Boris's advisers allowed him to stay for lunch

but you could guarantee that nearly everyone you met would live in the constituency. The idea was that he would pop into various businesses to encourage them to put up a special poster we had designed, based on the famous Kitchener 'Your country needs you' poster (see page 268). The visit was a huge success: lots of businesses put up the posters and Boris delivered an impromptu speech while standing on a bench to a crowd that had gathered. Afterwards we retired to a local café to speak to the media. Boris turned wistfully to his advisers and asked if there was any time in the programme for some lunch. When he got the answer he was looking for, the owner promptly produced the largest plate of liver, onions and mash I have ever seen, which the mayor set about demolishing.

Periodically, he would stop and claim he couldn't eat any more, but a few minutes later he'd launch another (doomed) attempt to clear the plate. Politicians and their promises...

Encouraging feedback from the media

We were joined fairly regularly by journalists who wanted to test the water in a marginal seat, but didn't want to travel too far from SW1. I would talk them through our strategy – in particular, the four discrete groups of voters we were targeting – and let them come canvassing with me so that they could hear what electors had to say (I would explain to the electors in question that I had a journalist with me and would promise that anything they said would not be publicly attributed to them).

This was clearly useful for the journalists concerned, but we often picked up useful feedback from them in return. For example, one person, who must remain anonymous, spent a couple of hours canvassing with Sarah and her team and then a couple of hours with us. As I drove them back to the station, they remarked that Labour had more people out than us, but they were simply calling on everyone in an area. In contrast, by this point in the campaign we were calling back on specific groups of voters who, this journalist could see from the conversations they had listened to, were going to decide the result of the election. This, and other conversations like it, was encouraging stuff to hear in the late stages of the campaign.

A policy that was making a difference on the doorsteps

The main parties had all published their manifestos, each full of hundreds of policy ideas. Most of these policies, however, made no difference whatsoever to the result of the election. Voters either didn't hear of them or, if they did, they weren't sufficient to shift people's votes.

There was one policy in our manifesto, however, that was making a difference on the doorsteps: our promise to give tenants of housing associations the right to buy their homes at a discount. Council tenants already had this right, but for the last thirty years most new social housing had been developed by housing associations and their tenants did not, which seemed unfair. We would put this right.

I suspect that if I had conducted a poll right across my constituency this would not have been one of our more popular policies. However, the people who didn't agree with it tended not to be Conservative supporters or, if they were, they didn't object to this policy strongly enough to change the way they voted. For people who lived in housing association properties, on the other hand, it was a vote-deciding issue. For many of them, it offered their only realistic chance of realising their dream of owning their own home. I remember being at East Croydon station one morning, handing out leaflets, when a man in his thirties came up to me and said, 'Can I just check something? If the Conservatives win, you're going to give people who live in housing association properties the right to buy their homes, yeah?'

'Yes,' I replied.

'Right, I'm voting for you,' he said and off he went.

The lesson was clear: in electoral terms, you should judge the effectiveness of a policy not on what percentage of people say they agree with it, but on how many votes switch as a result of it.

Going negative?

Almost all of the literature we put out during the eleven-month campaign was positive, making little or no mention of Sarah Jones or Labour. As the campaign drew to a close, however, we were conscious of the large number of people who were telling us that they still hadn't made up their minds. We therefore decided to produce a leaflet that would compare Sarah's and my views on one side and David Cameron's and Ed Miliband's views on the other (see pages 266–7). At the top of both sides we put 'Not sure who to vote for yet?' to make it clear who the leaflet was aimed at and we didn't include any party-political branding because we wanted as many people as possible to pick it up and start reading it (all literature distributed on behalf of a candidate during an election campaign is legally required to include an imprint saying who it is from, though, so if you read the small print you could work it out).

On 18 April, we delivered a leaflet through every one of the just under 50,000 letterboxes in Croydon Central in just over three hours

With the help of nearly 200 volunteers, we delivered this leaflet to every home in the constituency in a single morning. It was inspiring to see so many people gathered in one place to support me.

Labour hated it. They took to Twitter en masse complaining it was negative campaigning. They weren't on very strong ground, however, because over the course of the campaign their leaflets had contained far more negative content than ours.

Some people think any negative campaigning is too much. Others employ it all the time. Everyone has to find their own 'line in the sand'. My view is that political campaigns should be broadly positive, but people are making a choice between several alternatives so you have to say something about what's wrong with your opponents' policies as well as why people should vote for you. The key tests are whether what you say is fair comment and whether it isn't overly personal. I felt this leaflet passed both those tests. Labour couldn't dispute any of the facts we had included.

Ultimately, however, it was the verdict of swing voters that mattered. If they thought the leaflet was too negative, it would make them less likely to vote for me. If they liked it and found the contrast between Sarah and me informative, it would hopefully make them more likely to vote for me. And as was often the case, the feedback on the doorsteps was very different from the reaction on Twitter. The leaflet was a hit.

Nate Silver has spoken

Nate Silver is an American statistician who correctly predicted the outcome of the 2012 US presidential election in all fifty states. Now he had teamed up with the electionforecast.co.uk website to try to do the same for all 650 constituencies in this election. With some trepidation, I looked to see what he thought of our prospects. He declared Croydon Central to be the closest race in the country.

The first votes are cast

On 17 April, the council started sending ballot papers to those people who had applied to vote by post. Councils provide political parties with a list of these people, so on Monday 20 April we switched our energies from canvassing to calling on definite and probable Conservative supporters and target voters who we knew had received their ballot paper by post.

Our purpose was two-fold: first, to check whether people had returned their ballot papers – every person we could cross off now was one less person that we would have to chase up on polling day, the moment in the campaign when we would be under the most pressure. Second, we wanted to convince the people who hadn't yet returned their ballot paper to put their cross by my name.

This was an important moment in the campaign because it was the first time we got a sense as to how people were actually voting. The response was encouraging, particularly from the Conservative/UKIP waverers.

Boris is back

On 23 April, the Mayor of London was back in town for his second visit. This one was arranged at the last minute – there was a gap in his programme and his team wanted him to do a walkabout in Croydon town centre. I was sceptical about how much this would benefit my campaign – the people who shop in Croydon come from a wide area, so relatively few of the voters we would meet would be from Croydon Central. That said, he'd done exactly what I wanted him to the last two times he had visited (once during the short campaign and once back in September to launch my campaign), so I was happy to oblige him this time. He was mobbed by the closest thing you get in politics to fans and I got to spend an hour taking photos for people on their mobile phones, which was a pleasant break from the usual rigours of the campaign.

False hope

On 24 April, the council started opening returned postal ballot papers. As discussed in Chapter 2, at this stage they don't count how many votes each candidate has received, just check that each vote is valid, but representatives of each candidate are allowed to observe the process and while they're doing that they can see a reasonable number of ballot papers and so get a sense of how their party is doing.

That morning, I kept checking my phone anxiously for any message from Jason Cummings, who was there as my observer. I also thought about what would constitute a good result.

The question was: were Conservative supporters more, equally or less likely than Labour supporters to vote by post? At most elections, you only get an overall result so you never know how well you did among postal voters compared with people who voted at a polling station on the day. At best, you get a rough estimate from your observers at the postal ballot openings.

The only exceptions are the elections for the Mayor of London and the Greater London Assembly, in which votes are counted electronically and rather than simply getting an overall result you get a result for each ward based on the votes cast on the day and a borough-wide result for postal votes. By aggregating the ward results and comparing them with the borough-wide postal vote result, you can see how you did among people who voted on the day compared with how you did among people who voted by post. At the last mayoral election in 2012, we had done a bit better, and Labour a bit worse, among postal voters. So it seemed likely that to be on course to win, I needed to be ahead by a decent amount among postal voters.

When Jason arrived, the figures were better than we could possibly have hoped. I was miles ahead on over 50 per cent of the vote. Jason said the Labour activists present had shared that assessment.

It was an emotional moment. For the first time in the campaign, I felt confident I was far enough ahead to be sure of winning. I didn't want anyone easing off, however, so we agreed that these figures should not be widely shared among our activists.

Which was fortunate, because my confidence turned out to be very much misplaced.

The Prime Minister comes to town

On 25 April, the Prime Minister of our country came to Croydon to campaign for me. It doesn't get much better than that.

He gave a speech at the Fairfield Halls setting out the Conservative Party's offer to people from black and minority ethnic (BME) communities. It was a speech I'd wanted him to give for a long time. I'd long since lost count of the number of times I had canvassed someone from a BME background and they had said something along the lines of 'I think you do a good job for Croydon, but is the Conservative Party on the side of people like me?' In his speech, the Prime Minister answered that question with an emphatic 'Yes'.

His message was quintessentially Conservative: 'I want this to be an opportunity country where no matter who you are or where you're from, whether you're black, white, Asian or mixed race ... you can make the most of your talents.' There was a clear repudiation, however, of the attitudes behind the notorious 'Tebbit test'.[26] In direct contrast to Norman Tebbit's depressing, analogue view of identity, the Prime Minister said:

---

26 In 1990, Norman Tebbit had told the *Los Angeles Times*, 'A large proportion of Britain's Asian population fail to pass the cricket test. Which side do they cheer for? It's an interesting test. Are you still harking back to where you came from or where you are?'

> We are a shining example of a country where multiple identities work – a country where you can be Welsh and Hindu and British; Northern Irish and Jewish and British; where you can wear a kilt and a turban; where you can wear a hijab covered in poppies; where you can support Man United, the Windies and Team GB all at the same time.

He pointed out the progress the Conservative Party has made – we were fielding more candidates from BME backgrounds at this election than any other party. This was not a speech that rested on its laurels, however. He set ambitious targets to be achieved by 2020: 20 per cent more people from BME communities in work; a 20 per cent increase in the take-up of apprenticeships by people from BME backgrounds; 20 per cent more students from BME communities going to university; 20,000 more BME entrepreneurs receiving a start-up loan to help them build their own business; 20 per cent of new recruits to the police and armed forces from BME backgrounds. And finally, because we needed to finish putting our own house in order too, a goal of 20 per cent of Conservative Party candidates in winnable seats to be from BME backgrounds. The Conservative Party had been the party of the first female Prime Minister, Cameron argued, and 'we're going to be the party of the first black or Asian PM ... and I look forward to that day in our country'.

Sadly, media coverage of the speech was dominated by a slip of the tongue when the Prime Minister talked about wanting people to support West Ham rather than his team, Aston Villa. It was a significant speech that deserved more serious coverage. I used my email bulletin to ensure as many people as possible in Croydon Central heard what he had to say.

Did it make a difference? One speech, however good, couldn't possibly transform BME voters' perceptions of the Conservative Party, but it was a speech I'd long wanted the leader of the party to deliver. I was thrilled that David Cameron had done so and doubly thrilled that he'd chosen Croydon as the venue.

After the speech, the Prime Minister met with the Groves family. Lillian Groves was a constituent of mine who had been killed outside her home in New Addington by a driver under the influence of illegal drugs. The law in relation to drug driving was flawed, so the driver was sentenced to just eight months in jail, serving only four months.

Lillian's parents Gary and Natasha and her aunt Michaela had come to see me to try to get the law changed. I had raised the issue at Prime Minister's Questions and the Prime Minister had invited them to meet him at No. 10. He listened to their story, promised to get the law changed and was as good as his word. It was lovely for the family to have the chance to meet him again to say thank you.

The Prime Minister also recorded a video in which he had a few nice things to say about me:

> Think of what [Gavin's] achieved over the last five years. Twenty million pounds for a new A&E ... Getting regeneration and money into Croydon after the riots ... He's a really hard-working Member of Parliament, he's a great man, he does a brilliant job. Please send him back to Westminster. I want him as part of my team.

The Prime Minister with members of the Groves family

If you're interested, you can watch the full video at www.gavinbarwell.com/videos.

My abiding memory of the visit, however, is the ten or fifteen minutes I got to spend with the Prime Minister before he delivered his speech. I was conscious that whatever pressure I was under, he was under a lot more. I therefore tried to be as upbeat as possible without misleading him, focusing on the progress we were making in winning back Conservative/UKIP waverers and the fact that the 'Miliband supported by the SNP' message was working.

We spoke about why we were struggling in outer London. We agreed that as well as demographic change (outer London was becoming both more deprived and more ethnically diverse), the decline in home ownership was a key factor. It was good to hear him talk about his plans to help more people own their own home if we won the election.

I gave him one suggestion of something he could do in the last few weeks that would help London marginals in particular. There were plenty of people in Croydon Central earning a bit above the higher-rate income tax threshold who weren't rich. We should make more of our plans to raise this threshold to £50,000, which would make them up to £100 a month better off.

Back to earth with a bang

Every day more returned postal ballot papers were being opened and every day our lead over Labour was shrinking. There was only one day when they had more votes than us and we went into polling day estimating we were 1,500 votes ahead. I would happily have settled for that before a single postal ballot paper was opened. The first few days of ballot openings had given me a false confidence, however. Having thought I was home and dry, I now had to face the fact that this election was far from over.

Final conversations on the doorstep

Now that we had finished calling on target voters who had been sent their ballot by post, we switched back to normal canvassing. It was getting difficult to decide which roads to canvass. We had done every road multiple times and I found myself thinking, 'I can't knock on that door again – I've spoken to that family three times in the last year.'

As any experienced campaigner will tell you, even when you've knocked on every door multiple times it doesn't stop some people contacting your headquarters to say, 'Labour are out here all the time, where are you?' These calls tended to come from the bits of the constituency close to Sarah's HQ, which was right by East Croydon station. We knew much of her help was from outside Croydon. It looked like many of them were arriving by train and therefore had to be sent out on foot, so they were hitting the area around her office much harder than the rest of the constituency.

We were also getting reports that Labour were attacking me personally on the doorstep, in particular over the fact that I hadn't spoken in Parliament for a year and a half. This was true, but it was because as a government whip I'm not allowed to speak in the chamber, which was a detail that, funnily enough, they weren't mentioning. This didn't worry me unduly – all the evidence suggested people thought I was a good MP, so if they were attacking me it was likely to hurt them more than me. I therefore didn't put out a leaflet to rebut it. In hindsight, however, I think it did have some impact.

Several clear patterns were emerging from all the canvassing. First, we were winning back support from UKIP. Second, we were doing very well among the British Indian community, which is concentrated in the Park Hill area. The word was clearly going round within that community to support me – on the doorstep, people were saying things like, 'I used to be Labour, but my friend says you're a great MP.' Third and most worryingly, the constituency was polarising. The Conservative areas were if anything more Conservative than in 2010, but Labour were doing well in their strong areas.

Some of the most moving conversations I had on the doorstep were with black voters. One that stands out is with a lady in Forestdale, who I would guess was in her early thirties. She invited me into her flat, we talked about local issues and she explained that she thought I was a great MP, but wasn't sure if she could vote for me because her family would be horrified if they ever found out. I had the same conversation time and time again, and every time it was encouraging and demoralising in equal measure. The fact that such people were even considering voting Conservative was a sign of the progress we'd made. The fact that it was such a huge hurdle for them to cross was a sign of how far we still had to go.

It's the economy, stupid

On 30 April, the Chancellor came to Croydon. The purpose of this visit was simple: to highlight how the government's long-term economic plan was benefiting the town.

We took him to the Stanhope Schroders development next to East Croydon station. In hi-vis jackets (all politicians love a hi-vis jacket), we toured the new homes that were being built on a site that has lain largely vacant for my whole life. Here was physical evidence literally rising from the ground of the difference this government's economic policies were making.

I've known George Osborne since we worked together in the Research Department in our early twenties, so I feel like I have a different relationship with him than I do with David Cameron. We had ten minutes at the end of the visit to talk about how the campaign was going. Like the Prime Minister, he was interested in why we were struggling in outer London. He wished me luck, said he

Visiting new housing being built on a site next to East Croydon station with the Chancellor

was looking forward to seeing me on 11 May and then he was off to another marginal seat and I was back to knocking on doors.

Good news is bad news

On 1 May, Michael Ashcroft published his final batch of constituency polls.

> The last ten surveys contain mixed news for all parties and some noteworthy results. Perhaps the most striking of these is in Croydon Central, where in a poll completed yesterday I found a four-point Conservative lead over Labour. This compares to a four-point Labour lead in March and a six-point Labour lead last October. The UKIP share in the seat has nearly halved, from 19 per cent to 10 per cent, since the October poll.

On the first voting intention question – 'If there was a general election tomorrow, which party would you vote for?' – there had been a complete turnaround in six weeks:

Conservatives	43 per cent (+10)
Labour	40 per cent (-1)
UKIP	10 per cent (-6)
Greens	4 per cent (-2)
Liberal Democrats	3 per cent (0)

(The figures in brackets show the change from the March 2015 poll)

The picture was similar, though not quite as dramatic, on the second question – 'Thinking specifically about your own parliamentary constituency at the next general election and the candidates who are likely to stand for election to Westminster there, which party's candidate do you think you will vote for in your own constituency?':

Conservatives	44 per cent (+7)
Labour	40 per cent (-1)
UKIP	10 per cent (-3)
Greens	3 per cent (-2)
Liberal Democrats	2 per cent (-1)

The number of people saying that they would definitely not vote Labour was up 4 percentage points at 43 per cent. The number saying they would definitely not vote Conservative was down 5 percentage points at 41 per cent. For the first time, more people were hostile to Labour than to us.

There had been a similar change when people were asked what kind of government they wanted to see after 7 May 2015:

A Conservative government	33 per cent (+5)
A Labour government	31 per cent (-4)
A coalition between the Conservatives and the Liberal Democrats	12 per cent (+1)
A coalition between Labour and the Liberal Democrats	10 per cent (-2)

David Cameron's lead over Ed Miliband had got even bigger. Thirty-seven per cent (up 6 points) were satisfied with the job he was doing overall as Prime Minister. Thirty-one per cent (down one) were dissatisfied and would prefer to have Ed Miliband as Prime Minister instead. Nineteen per cent (down four) were dissatisfied, but would still prefer to have him as Prime Minister than Ed Miliband.

Economic optimism had increased even further: 68 per cent thought the economy would fare well over the next year for them and their family, compared with 25 per cent who thought it would fare badly.

Seventy-nine per cent (up 8 points) of 2010 Conservative voters were now planning to vote Conservative again, with 8 per cent (down 7) planning to switch to UKIP and 9 per cent (down 2) to Labour. Eighty-three per cent (down 2) of 2010 Labour voters were still planning to vote Labour with 10 per cent (unchanged) planning to switch to me and 3 per cent (up 1) to UKIP. That meant there was still virtually no direct swing from us to Labour. However, we were now doing better than Labour among the 2010 Liberal Democrats. Forty-one per cent (up 10 points) were planning to vote for me compared with 34 per cent (up 1) for Labour. I was suspicious of this latter finding – it didn't match what we were finding on the doorstep – so I suspected that we were not as far ahead as this poll implied.

Finally, with just six days to go Labour were beating us on local activity, but not by much. Seventy-three per cent of those polled had been contacted over the last few weeks by us and 84 per cent by Labour.

Most of our activists were euphoric; I was concerned.[27] Although I felt things were moving our way, our canvassing did not suggest we were 4 points ahead. We had only been 6 points

27 You may by now be forming the impression that there is no result of a poll with which I would be happy.

ahead in 2010 and Labour and UKIP were certainly doing better now than they had then. My fear was that if people thought the result was in the bag, they'd ease off and we could be pipped at the post.

Squeezing UKIP till the pips squeaked

The Ashcroft poll showed that we'd had real success squeezing the UKIP vote, but we felt there was still more there if we squeezed harder. We were using the bookies' odds as evidence that UKIP couldn't win in Croydon Central and that argument had just been endorsed by none other than the UKIP candidate, Peter Staveley, who admitted that the best he could do was come third.

So we decided to do a mailing to Conservative/UKIP waverers and core UKIP supporters (on the doorstep, even some of them were beginning to move our way). Rather than have it coming from me, however, we asked our candidate in South Thanet, Craig Mackinlay, to write it. Craig was a former deputy leader of UKIP, so the message would have much more credibility coming from him. This is what he said:

> My name is Craig Mackinlay. I used to be the Deputy Leader of UKIP and stood as a parliamentary candidate for them in the 1997, 2001 and 2005 general elections.
>
> However, I'm writing to ask you to vote for your local Conservative candidate, Gavin Barwell, on Thursday. Why?
>
> First, because Gavin has consistently voted for a referendum on our membership of the EU, while his Labour opponent Sarah Jones says she is happy with the EU as it is and doesn't support a referendum.
>
> And second because the constituency in which you live is a two-horse race between Labour and the Conservatives. The bookies make UKIP 100/1 outsiders. Their candidate Peter Staveley has admitted he can't win saying 'the best I can get is third [place]'

> (see http://www.croydonadvertiser.co.uk/Ukip-candidate-campaigning-Croydon-Central-says-s/story-26409634-detail/story.html#foQFzJU5Vv6mdaAX.03).
>
> If, like me, you're not happy with the EU and want change, it's essential that you don't waste your vote by supporting a candidate who has no chance of winning. Please vote for Gavin Barwell to make sure we have enough MPs in the next parliament who will let the British people decide on our future in Europe.

A number of Conservative/UKIP waverers referred to this letter on polling day, so it clearly had some effect.

The pursuit of happiness

On the evening of 1 May, I attended an event at Croydon Conference Centre. The guest speaker was Chris Gardner, the American entrepreneur, author and philanthropist whose autobiography, *The Pursuit of Happyness*, was the inspiration for the film of the same title, in which Will Smith starred as Gardner.

Chris gave one of the most inspiring speeches I have ever heard, based around his incredible life story. He had clearly taken some interest in our election and invited me on stage to explain what motivated me. It was a great opportunity to speak to a diverse audience that would never have come to a political meeting, but above all an honour to meet someone who is an inspiration to so many.

Manic Monday

On Monday 4 May, we were joined by Michael Gove, Francis Maude and a coach full of special advisers. This was the only day that our logistics broke down. It was a bank holiday: the pub we went to for lunch was already busy and couldn't cope with another forty or so people turning up at once. The result was quite a few people spending a couple of hours in a beer garden waiting for their food when I desperately wanted them out on the streets.

Later in the day, we were joined by Sol Campbell, the former England international footballer. It was one of the more surreal moments of the campaign. Sol was interested in being the next Conservative candidate for Mayor of London and was helping out in a number of our target seats in the capital. After a brief discussion about his 'goal that never was' against Argentina in the 1998 World Cup and the obligatory photo to tweet, he took a team off to hand out leaflets to people at East Croydon station.

The surreal moments in a campaign are just moments. The reality is hour after hour of knocking on doors. As soon as Sol left, I was back at it with Michael Gove still in tow. I knocked on the door of a teacher, who was upset with the government's education reforms. With some trepidation, I invited Michael over. After he left, the lady said, 'He's completely different from what

© Greg Hands MP

A surreal moment: campaigning with football legend Sol Campbell

I expected.' She still didn't agree with some of his policies, but a brief conversation certainly changed her perception of Michael and how he regarded teachers. As a candidate in an individual constituency, I can at least try to talk face to face with all the people I am asking to vote for me. When you're a Cabinet minister you can't communicate what you're trying to do and why you're doing it with all the people affected face to face; you have to rely on what the media reports or what unions tell their members and therein lies the problem.

Later that evening, as the rain began to fall I canvassed my final house of the campaign. They were undecided.

The difference a good MP makes

Polling day was now just two days away. Work was already underway preparing the lists of people we would be trying to contact on the day, so there was no point doing any more canvassing – any new Conservatives or target voters we found wouldn't make it onto those lists. Instead, we decided to spend the day touring the constituency, filming short clips about my achievements over the last five years (the inspiration for this idea came from Sarah Jones, who had done a 24-hour tour of the constituency in March). We would live-tweet the video clips during the day and also edit them together into a video to be emailed out to everyone on our distribution list, called 'The Difference a Good Local MP Makes'. You can watch the video at www.gavinbarwell.com/videos.

It's fair to say that this was only a partial success. The people we emailed the video to the next day liked it. On Twitter, however, a large number of Crystal Palace fans were furious that I'd claimed to have saved the club from liquidation. Except I hadn't said this at all. If they'd watched the video, they'd have seen that I only claimed to have played 'a small part' in helping the club's fans lobby the coalition government and Lloyds TSB.

What had happened was a classic example of the internet on a bad day. A Labour supporter by the name of Jon Ellacott had gone onto one of the fan forums saying I was claiming to have single-handedly saved the club. Within minutes a virtual mob had formed. Once that happens, there's really nothing you can do but ignore your Twitter feed for twenty-four hours. It was ironic because back in 2010 I'd received hundreds of emails from Palace fans thanking me for what I'd done (which, I'll repeat here, was nothing more than to support their efforts to save the club). That's Twitter for you.

The last video clip was of me with Boris Johnson, who had come to support me for the third time in the campaign and brought an army of activists with him. Once we'd recorded the video, we sent everyone out leafleting in the Addiscombe and Park Hill areas, the part of the constituency that Labour was working hardest.

Dedication's what you need

On the evening before polling day, we planned to deliver a personalised card to all definite and probable Conservative supporters and target voters other than those who we knew had voted by post. It would tell them where they had to go to vote the next day. It would also include a simple message that varied depending on their voting intention (for example, if they were undecided but preferred David Cameron to Ed Miliband, the message would be that if they wanted David to be Prime Minister they needed to vote for me; if, on the other hand, they were a strong Conservative, the focus would be on electing a Conservative government). In the case of the two groups of target voters who we thought would determine the eventual result – Conservative/UKIP waverers and those people who were undecided between David Cameron and Ed Miliband but wanted to keep me as their local MP – we would knock on their door to try to have a conversation with them and hand them their card, rather than just posting it through their letterbox.

This was a hugely ambitious plan, requiring at least 150 activists from 6 p.m. to 9 p.m. and perfect logistics. In the end, we nearly pulled it off. We didn't manage to knock on all the doors we wanted to, but we did have lots of very useful conversations. A couple of activists weren't listening when we explained that these cards were addressed to specific electors and so tried to deliver one to every home in the roads they were given (and hence ran out of cards) rather than delivering the right cards to the right people. Not ideal, but overall it was an impressive effort.

I was one of four people calling on those who were undecided, had no preference between David Cameron and Ed Miliband but wanted to keep me as their MP (the others being one of my best friends, Mark; Neil O'Brien, who is one of George Osborne's special advisers; and Tina Stowell, the leader of the House of Lords). I gave up at about 9.15 p.m. when my visits were starting to seem less 'hopeful MP dropping round' and more 'scary night-time caller'.

I caught up with Tina. She was upset – she felt she'd let me down because she hadn't been able to call on everyone in the time available. I couldn't believe it. Here was a Cabinet minister delivering leaflets on her own at 9.30 at night, on the fifth or sixth occasion she had come to help me, and she felt she hadn't done enough!

As Roy Castle sang, 'If you want beat the rest, dedication's what you need.' Whatever else could be said about this campaign, one thing was for sure: Tina Stowell is a legend.

Still on message

The last thing I did before getting some sleep in advance of the most gruelling day of the campaign was to send an email to everyone on my distribution list:

> How you vote on 7 May will decide two things.
>
> First, who runs the country for the next five years.

One of two people is going to be Prime Minister after the election – David Cameron or Ed Miliband.

With the SNP projected to win nearly every seat in Scotland, there's no chance of Labour winning an overall majority. If Ed Miliband does become PM, it will be with the support of Alex Salmond and Nicola Sturgeon.

So what would you prefer – David Cameron or Ed Miliband dependent on the SNP? Who do you want representing Britain in Europe: David Cameron, who will renegotiate our relationship and then give us a referendum – or Ed Miliband, who is happy with the EU as it is? Who do you trust to run our economy: David Cameron, who is sorting out the mess Labour left us in – or Ed Miliband, who still doesn't accept the last Labour government spent too much?

You may think neither is perfect, but if you prefer David Cameron you need to vote for me. If Labour win here, Ed Miliband will probably make it to No. 10 – and according to the bookies I'm the only person in with a chance of stopping them.

But as well as choosing who runs the country for the next five years, you're also choosing who you want to be your MP.

It's been an honour to do the job for the last five years. I've lived in Croydon my whole life and I'm incredibly passionate about it. I hope you feel I've done a good job. I got funding from the government and Boris to rebuild after the riots, I helped bring Westfield here and I recently secured a new A&E department at our local hospital. I've also helped thousands of individual constituents with their problems, given 200 local young people work experience in my office and done my best to keep in touch with the people I work for (through these email bulletins for example).

But there's so much more to do – making sure the Westfield development gets underway as soon as possible, regenerating district centres like Central Parade and Portland Road and moving East Croydon station to zone 4 to save commuters money. Unlike any of my opponents, I've published a detailed vision for the future of our town.

Finally a word about my values. I got involved in politics to build a fairer society. I'm sure the other candidates vying for your vote did too – we just disagree about what a fair society looks like or what policies will deliver one.

To me fairness is about ensuring there's a job for everyone who wants one. Labour care about unemployment too, but their policies tend to increase it. Every Labour government there's ever been has left office with more people out of work than when they came to power. Under this government, unemployment in Croydon Central has halved.

Fairness is about ensuring people get paid a decent wage for a hard day's work. That's why I've supported increases in the minimum wage and back the Living Wage.

Fairness is about ensuring everyone pays their fair share in tax. This year, the richest 1 per cent will pay a higher share of income tax – and the poorest 50 per cent a lower share – than in any year of the last Labour government.

Fairness is about ensuring that work pays. That's why a Conservative government will increase the personal allowance and the 40p threshold so you can keep more of the money you work hard to earn. It's why I've supported a cap on the amount of benefits out-of-work families can receive – under Labour, some were getting over £50,000 a year. And it's why I support measures to help people own their own home – and oppose our Labour council's plan for half of all new homes built to be council or housing association homes, which will make it harder for people to get on the housing ladder.

Fairness is about ensuring all children get a good start in life. That's why I've backed the closure of schools that are letting our children down – and why I value teachers so highly.

Fairness is about dignity in retirement. That's why I've supported increases in the state pension, the protection of pensioner benefits like the Freedom Pass and a cap on care costs.

And fairness is about not having to worry about the cost of treatment if we get sick or have an accident. The NHS saved my life when

> I had cancer as a child and gave outstanding care to my dad when he was dying of Alzheimer's. It's one of the best things about this country and I will always protect it.
>
> So that's my pitch. It's been an honour to work for you for the last five years. Whether I continue is down to you.

The key test of any political strategy is how it survives contact with the enemy. Looking back, it's remarkable how closely the email above reflects the strategy we had agreed eleven months earlier. The only difference – and it's a subtle though significant one – is that the choice of Prime Minister is no longer framed as being between David Cameron and Ed Miliband, but between David Cameron and Ed Miliband supported by the SNP. Everything else – the focus on who should be Prime Minister and whether I should continue as the local MP, the positioning on the centre ground, the negating of Labour's message on the NHS and the emphasis on my plan for the future of Croydon – is unchanged.

It's almost as if we knew what we were doing. The question was: would it be enough to win?

Chapter 22

Polling day

POLLING DAY. IN the end, all campaigns come down to it. The final fifteen hours before the battle's lost and won. And when the polls close at 10 p.m., you're not finished. Within minutes, the count gets underway. In a political campaign, it's the longest day.

The productivity challenge

Twelve months before, Labour had wiped the floor with us on polling day. On Twitter, their London regional director was boasting about how they planned to do the same again. They had set themselves the target of getting 500 activists from across south London onto the streets of Croydon Central.

After asking everyone we could think of – and, let's be honest, begging – we were confident we would have over 300 people knocking up. This was far more than we had ever had before, but still 200 fewer than Labour were hoping to have. We needed a plan to bridge the gap by making better use of the people we had.

To explain the plan we came up with, it's helpful to understand what we normally do on polling day. By this stage of the campaign, we've given up trying to talk round opposition supporters or speak to people we haven't been able to canvass yet. The focus now is on what the Americans call GOTV (get out the vote): ensuring the people who've told us they are likely to vote for us actually do so. In an ideal world, this involves four things.

First, we put 'tellers' outside every polling station. Their job is to ask everyone who comes to vote for their electoral roll number (which is on the polling card that most people bring with them) or their name and address if they don't have their roll number.

Second, the information our tellers gather is relayed back to our campaign centre in that area, which is normally the home of one of our supporters. In a local election, we would have a campaign centre for each target ward; in a general election, we might have several campaign centres in each constituency. Once the data on who has voted has got to the campaign centre, it is cross-referenced against the list of people we are trying to get out to vote. If any of these people have voted, we cross them off the list.

Third, the person in charge of the campaign centre then sends out volunteers to call on our potential supporters who have not yet voted to encourage them to do so. This is known as 'knocking up'. Those people who tell us they've voted, they're going to vote later or they're not going to vote can be crossed off our list. If no one is in, we leave a leaflet saying it's polling day. And we keep knocking up until everyone is crossed off our list. Normally, we only knock up people who have told us they are going to vote Conservative. However, if we get to early May and we haven't found enough definite Conservatives to be confident of winning, we might add people who have told us they are *probably* going to vote Conservative or people that CCHQ's voter model predicts are *likely* to be Conservative supporters.

The final thing we need is a small team of drivers to take potential supporters who are unwell or relatively immobile to their polling station.

This ideal operation requires a huge amount of manpower. If we're short of people, we do what's known as a 'blind knock-up' where we forget about the telling and use everyone we have to knock up. We'll waste a bit of time calling on people who have already voted, but we'll still cover more ground than if we used most of our manpower telling and therefore had only a handful of people knocking up.

The key point here is that while telling provides useful intelligence that can reduce the amount of knocking up we have to do, it does not on its own increase the Conservative vote. It is knocking on people's doors, reminding them that it's polling day, persuading those who still haven't made up their minds to go our way and arranging lifts for those who need them that make a difference.

Even with a blind knock-up, though, precious time is often wasted. The knocking-up teams are usually given an hour or two's work at a time and therefore have to keep travelling back and forth to the campaign centre to get more work. There is absolutely no reason why this should happen – the list of people to knock up isn't being updated with information from tellers. It is simply force of habit.

Furthermore, anyone who has ever helped on polling day for a general election will tell you that most of the people you knock up were going to vote for you anyway. You have relatively few conversations where you feel that you changed someone's mind. When it's a council election, many people won't know it's polling day so the simple act of reminding them makes a big difference, but the wall-to-wall media coverage and avalanche of literature you get in a marginal constituency makes it pretty hard not to know when there's a general election on.

To try to make maximum use of the people we had, we therefore made three changes to our normal polling day plan.

The first change was who we knocked up. Because we thought the result was going to be very close, we wanted to knock up key floating voters – the undecideds who preferred David Cameron to Ed Miliband as Prime Minister or who wanted me as their MP, Liberal Democrats who preferred us to Labour, Conservatives tempted by UKIP, and even solid UKIP supporters. If we knocked up all of these on top of our definite and likely Conservative voters, though, we'd have to call on over 25,000 people. We simply didn't have the manpower for that.

We therefore decided not to knock up people who we had canvassed as strong Conservatives since May 2014 (i.e. since we had been specifically testing whether people were tempted by UKIP) and who had voted in that year's elections. The theory was that if we were sure they were Conservatives and we knew they had voted even in a low-turnout election, we didn't need to knock on their door – they would vote for us anyway. Put simply, we wanted our knocking-up teams to focus on speaking to people who might need some persuading.

The second change was not to use anyone as a teller who was willing to knock up. What mattered was talking to as many potential supporters as possible, not standing outside polling stations modelling blue rosettes. There were some people who either wouldn't or physically couldn't knock up – we would use them to tell in our best areas. In the rest of the constituency, however, we would do a blind knock-up.

The final change was to do away with people going back and forth to a campaign centre. We would divide the constituency into twenty-seven sectors and appoint an experienced activist as team leader in each sector. In the more Conservative parts of the constituency, a sector might equate to one polling district.[28] In the less Conservative areas it might be two polling districts. Each team leader would hold the master list of our potential supporters in their sector and lead a team of volunteers knocking up those people. If we were telling in their polling district/s, they would periodically collect data from the tellers and cross off anyone on their list who had voted.[29]

With one exception, everyone would spend the whole day – apart from lunch, which we would organise at a central venue – out on the streets. The exception was Tim Pollard. He would liaise with the team leaders during the day to monitor what proportion of their list they had crossed off and reallocate resources between them accordingly. Those people who couldn't join us for the whole day would be given Tim's number to call when they were on their way. Rather than coming to a campaign centre and then being sent on somewhere to knock up (another waste of time), they would be directed straight to one of the team leaders.

I wouldn't be assigned to any of the teams. Instead I would move from sector to sector accompanied by some close friends and family members, whose job was to try to keep me relaxed as well as helping with the knocking up.

This plan was the brainchild of Jason Cummings. I loved the idea of doing away with trooping back and forth to a campaign centre and only using people who would not knock up for telling, but I took some convincing not to call on Conservatives who had voted in the low-turnout elections twelve months before. In the end, Jason talked me round. The only change to the plan I made was to introduce a team of Indian activists knocking up

---

28 A polling district is a sub-division of a council ward. Each district has its own polling station, where the electors who live in that district have to go to vote on polling day (unless they vote by post or proxy). In Croydon, the average polling district has just under 2,000 electors.

29 If you're wondering why the tellers couldn't just email the data to the team leaders, bear in mind that our tellers were people who were no longer physically up to pounding the streets, generally due to old age – most of them weren't regular users of smartphones.

Indian target voters and a team of Tamil activists knocking up Tamil target voters.

We had our plan: it was time for the big day.

Not the best start...

Some campaigns start polling day at 4 a.m. with a dawn raid. The idea is to deliver a 'Good morning, it's polling day' leaflet through the door of all your potential supporters before anyone leaves home to encourage people to vote on their way to work.

While I'm as keen on flogging myself to death in an attempt to win elections as the next candidate – actually, more so – experience has taught me that dawn raids are counter-productive. Every time I've seen them tried, the result is all your key activists are dead on their feet by early evening. Right at that point at which your effort should be reaching a peak, people start giving up, exhausted. Far better, I felt, to let everyone have a lie-in and a nice breakfast and start knocking on doors at 10 a.m., so that they could go through to close of poll at 10 p.m. We therefore started the day with a breakfast briefing for our team leaders at the Harvester in Addington Village.

As I was parking my car, my mind was on other things and I managed to scrape the car next to me. I was furious with myself. Now, when I should be briefing our team leaders I was going to have to wander round the pub to find whose car I had damaged. Fortunately – at least from my point of view – it turned out to belong to Helen Pollard, Tim's wife. She told me not to worry about it and we sorted it all out once the election was out of the way.

Knocking up

I was joined for the day by my brother Richard; two of my best friends, Barry and Mark (the rest are Labour voters and therefore not all that keen on canvassing for a Tory); and Scott Colvin, who used to work with me at Conservative Central Office.

We started on Woodmere Avenue and the roads off it in Ashburton ward, a strongly Conservative area with some UKIP leanings. The response was very encouraging. Everyone we spoke to, whether they had been canvassed as Conservative supporters or floating voters, had voted for me or was going to vote for me apart from one person who had been canvassed as undecided but wanting me to continue as the MP. She said she had never voted Conservative in her life and couldn't bring herself to do so this time.

At the end of the session, I checked my emails and found this from another elector we had canvassed as undecided but wanting me to continue as her MP:

> Dear Gavin,
>
> I cast my vote promptly this morning about 8.45. I voted for you – I broke the pattern of a lifetime! I'm not a Tory, but I wanted you to remain my MP. You have done a great job over the last five years. I don't know what will happen tonight when the votes are counted, but I just want to say thank you for all your hard work and for making a difference for Croydon.

You win some, you lose some...

Then it was off to Oaks Farm for a quick lunch and a debrief with the team leaders. In our strong areas, the response was very good – virtually everyone on our list was saying they were going to vote for me. In Addiscombe, Woodside and parts of the town centre, we were finding relatively few people at home. In Fieldway and New Addington, there was a huge amount of Labour activity, but it seemed surprisingly untargeted – cars driving round with loudspeakers reminding our supporters as well as theirs that it was polling day. In light of this, we decided to move resources out of our best areas, initially to those two wards and then later in the afternoon to Addiscombe and Woodside.

After lunch my team headed to Featherbed Lane and the roads off it in Addington. This was quite a good area for us, though not as strong as the Woodmere Avenue area because it was even more UKIP leaning. Again, the response was very encouraging. Then we went up to New Addington to join the push there. Here, the response was not as good, though still not bad. The Conservative/UKIP waverers were dividing 50/50 between us and UKIP and our canvassing wasn't as accurate as elsewhere – some people who had been recorded as potential Conservatives turned out to be lifelong Labour voters. We bumped into a team of Labour activists for the first time. Once again, the downside of them having so much outside help was clear – they looked like they didn't know where they were and seemed to wander around fairly aimlessly.

By now it was late afternoon. We had large numbers of people working in New Addington, so my team moved to Regency Walk in Shirley, another area that was pretty good for us but with UKIP leanings. Richard and Scott had to leave; they were replaced by my wife Karen and Barry's wife Lucia. The response here was very encouraging, more akin to the Woodmere Avenue and Featherbed Lane areas than New Addington.

At about 6 p.m., we sent out the final email bulletin of the campaign, a short video of Boris, which we had recorded on Tuesday night. The message was simple: 'Folks, this is it. We are now in the last few hours of the election campaign. You can make a difference in Croydon Central and get your superb MP Gavin Barwell re-elected. Get out to vote now, folks, you know it makes sense.'

Then we were off to the Bingham Road area of Ashburton ward, an area I had long felt was a bellwether for the whole constituency. The floating voters here were dividing pretty evenly between us and Labour, but what was encouraging was the large number of Conservative activists we saw in neighbouring roads. In this crucial area, at this crucial time, we were outnumbering Labour on the ground.

By now it was about 8.30 p.m. We hit one last area – Grant Road and the surrounding roads in Addiscombe ward – then called stumps just before 9.30. The polls were still open for another half an hour, but most people were no longer opening their doors and those who did were starting to get annoyed at being disturbed at that time of night. We weren't going to get anyone else out to vote.

And that was it.

For the last year, this campaign had dominated all my waking hours and disturbed my sleeping ones. Now it was over. In a few hours' time, I would find out whether it had all been worth it.

The response on the doorstep had felt good. The people we'd canvassed as Conservatives had nearly all voted for us. So had the people we'd canvassed as Conservative/UKIP waverers. And we'd done well among the probable Conservatives and the undecideds who preferred Cameron to Miliband or wanted to keep me as their MP, particularly in the more Conservative parts of the constituency. I was confident that I would get more votes than I had in 2010. The question was: would that be enough?

The problem was we had no idea how well the Labour vote had turned out. When you're telling, you can keep a running total of how many of your potential supporters have voted versus how many other people, giving you a pretty good idea of the result, at least in areas where it is a two-horse race. When you're doing a blind knock-up, however – as we were in all but the most Conservative areas – you get very little feel for how your opponents' votes are turning out. If the Liberal Democrat and Green votes completely collapsed, I could do quite a bit better than in 2010 and still lose.

I'd have a better idea when the exit poll was published just after 10 p.m.

A night at home with my mates

With the polls closed, the count could begin.

I enjoy polling day, but I hate counts. I always have done. When each ballot box arrives, the clerks count the number of ballot papers in the box, checking it matches the number of ballot papers issued at the relevant polling station to ensure that there's been no fraud. At this point, they're not counting the number of votes per candidate, just the total number of ballot papers. While this is going on, however, you can see a good sample of the ballot papers. Unless it's very close, you can tell who's won. The clerks then spend hours counting the number of votes per candidate. You stand around with very little to do, surrounded by people who are exhausted and either understandably upset, a bit gloaty or very stressed. Take it from me, counts are truly awful occasions.

I had therefore formulated a cunning plan. I would stay at home, order a curry and watch the results with my closest friends – Barry, who had been with me all day, and Atul, Paul and Pete, who were Labour supporters and so obviously hadn't, but wanted to be with me when the result came through. My campaign manager Ian would give me a call when he had anything to report (I suspected the first call was going to be, 'It's too close to call...'). I would only turn up at the count five minutes before the returning officer declared the result.

My two eldest children – Jack and Sam, who were twelve and nine – were desperate to come to the declaration. I wanted them there too if I won. After all, this might be their only chance to see me win – if the seat continued to move against us demographically the 2020 election would be an uphill struggle whatever the national picture. I didn't want them to come if I lost, however – I thought they'd find it too upsetting. So Karen packed them off to bed, promising that we would wake them up if I won. We settled down in front of the TV and awaited the exit poll.

When it was announced, it suggested we were going to do better than I expected. The BBC were predicting that we would win 316 seats, 9 more than we had won in 2010 and just short of an overall majority. Labour were predicted to win 239, 19 fewer than they had won in 2010; the Liberal Democrats just 10, 47 fewer than in 2010. The poll also suggested that the SNP would win a remarkable fifty-eight of the fifty-nine seats in Scotland. My boss, Michael Gove, was visibly shocked. Paddy Ashdown said he would eat his hat if it proved accurate.[30]

The actual results, once they started coming in, were even better for the Conservatives than the exit poll suggested. The moment I started to believe the exit poll was when Marcus Jones increased his majority in Nuneaton, a key West Midlands Conservative/Labour marginal that we had only won by 2,000 votes in 2010. As well as doing well against Labour, we also seemed to be winning every Liberal Democrat seat in the south-west. Amazingly, it began to look like we would win an overall majority. If we were doing this well nationally, surely I would be OK?

My phone rang. It was Jason, who was at the count. They had done a tally when the ballot paper numbers were checked and they thought I had won by about 1,000. However, it was too close to be certain. That brought me down to earth with a bump. Then I saw on the news that Labour had gained Ealing Central & Acton, an outer London marginal very similar to mine. Whatever was happening nationally, Croydon Central was clearly going to be a nail-biter.

The rest of the night was a bit of a haze. I'm pretty sure the Ilford North declaration was before mine. This was another Labour gain in outer London – and in a seat that hadn't been considered a marginal. It was clear that the one part of the country where Labour were doing well against us was outer London (they would also gain Brentford & Isleworth and Enfield North, another seat

30 It didn't – the Liberal Democrats ended up winning just eight seats, two fewer seats than predicted.

that was very similar to mine, but I don't remember hearing these results on the night).

At about 4 a.m., Jason called again to say the count was nearly finished. It looked incredibly tight, but they thought I was just ahead. Then another call: it wasn't finished at all. The returning officer's provisional declaration was that I had won by 167 votes, but Labour had (understandably) asked for a recount. Another call about an hour later: it still looked very close. I suggested to Jason that he might not want to call again until he had some actual news to report (I think the exact language I used was rather more colourful – sorry, Jason).

The next ninety minutes were not ones I would care to repeat. At the risk of sounding selfish, if there was a swing to Labour and I was one of forty or fifty Conservative MPs to lose their seats, I could take that. To lose my seat on the same day the party was winning an overall majority, however, would be incredibly tough.

I phoned the returning officer, Nathan Elvery, and explained that I was only five minutes away and that I wanted to bring my eldest two children if I had won, but not if I had lost. I asked if he could give me an indication before I set off for the Fairfield Halls. He agreed to do so, something I will always be grateful for.

The fat lady sings

Time went by so slowly.

Shortly before 6 a.m., I got another call. This time it was Ian. He had the final result. I had won by 165 votes, one of the slimmest margins in the entire country. To put the margin in context, if just two people in each polling district had switched from Conservative to Labour, I would have lost.

The best moment of that night was waking Jack and Sam. As soon as they opened their eyes, they knew what it meant. I then gave my mum a call to tell her the result and to meet us at the Fairfield Halls and off we went.

When we got there, I went straight onto the stage for the declaration:

Barwell, Gavin (Conservative)	22,753 votes	ELECTED
Jones, Sarah (Labour)	22,588 votes	
Staveley, Peter (UKIP)	4,810 votes	
Sutton, Esther (Green)	1,454 votes	
Fearnley, James (Liberal Democrat)	1,152 votes	
Ashley, April (Trade Union & Socialist Coalition)	127 votes	
Camden, Martin (UK Progressive Democracy Party)	57 votes	

Despite UKIP getting 9 per cent of the vote and despite all the difficult choices we'd had to take in government, I had got more than 3,000 more votes than in 2010. Across the country as a whole, we had increased our vote share by 0.7 percentage points. In London, it had gone up by just 0.3 points. My own share, however, had gone up by more than 3.5 points. I had got more votes than any Conservative candidate in Croydon Central since 1979.

Even that, though, had only been enough by a whisker. The Liberal Democrat vote had collapsed, which was no reflection on their candidate, James Fearnley, who is a real talent. Partially as a result of this, Sarah Jones had got nearly 6,000 more votes than her predecessor, Gerry Ryan, in 2010 and had increased the Labour share of the vote by more than 9 percentage points, substantially better than Labour had managed either in London overall (7 points) or across the country as a whole (1.5 percentage points). She had got more votes than any Labour candidate in Croydon Central since Geraint Davies (now the MP for Swansea West) in 1997.

The truth was it was a very good result for both main parties.

Sarah looked devastated, as I would have in her position. I could probably understand better than anyone what she must be feeling. To work hard and lose is tough, but to lose by such a small amount is even tougher because you inevitably think,

'If only I had done...' I'm sure it was small comfort, if any, but in my speech I paid tribute to her and her campaign team. I don't share their values, but I admire anyone who gives up their time to fight for what they believe in.

I thanked those who had voted for me and particularly those who had given up their time to help me win. Conscious that I had only won by a handful of votes, however, I also spoke to those who had voted for Sarah. I reassured them that I would work with Steve Reed, Chris Philp and our Labour council to do what was best for the town and try to ensure that everyone benefited from the economic recovery.

To be honest, it wasn't my best speech. I'd spent much more time working on the alternative version since that would have been the last thing I would say in public life. Still, it hopefully got

© Tim Pollard

With my wife and eldest two boys, Jack and Sam, after the declaration across my sincere gratitude and desire to listen to and represent all my constituents, whoever they had voted for.

After the declaration there were hugs for some of the people who had made this victory possible and a round of media interviews – the national broadcasters, the *Evening Standard* and the local papers. Someone got some nice pictures of Karen, Jack, Sam and me, which made it onto London news bulletins. Their friends were very impressed they were on TV.

At about 7 a.m., it was time to go home. Karen was exhausted and went straight to bed. I couldn't sleep, however. I wasn't euphoric, just... awake. Which was lucky, because there was one final debate to be had. Jack had missed his bus to school and was strongly of the view that this meant he should have the day off. I drove him to school. Michael Gove would have been proud of me.

Chapter 23

Coming down

The day after the night before

THE REST OF Friday was spent responding to emails and text messages from family, friends, people who had helped with the campaign and constituents who were pleased I was still their MP. I was touched to get texts from George Osborne, Michael Gove and Boris Johnson.

And for once there were some nice messages on Twitter too. I particularly appreciated those from constituents who hadn't been involved with the campaign:

> Well deserved win by Gavin Barwell in Croydon Central. Most hard working MP I've known since coming to Croydon 50 years ago
>
> – PETER KEIK

> Congratulations @BackBarwell, first time voted #Tory, and glad that I did. Looking forward to a more prosperous Croydon #hardworkingMP
>
> – Imran Aziz

> Congratulations to Gavin Barwell, been very impressed with his attitude. Won our household over hands down
>
> – Tony Long

But perhaps the tweet that meant the most to me was from Andrew Cooper, the Prime Minister's former director of strategy and founder of the polling company Populus:

> @BackBarwell re-elected: one of the highlights of the night. One of the best & brightest. No one else would have held Croydon Central.

Andrew's a former Croydon Central resident so he knows the constituency well and few people have a better understanding of British public opinion. This was high praise indeed.

Even Inside Croydon, possibly my most enthusiastic critics, managed something approaching a compliment:

> Barwell is a strong incumbent with the professional campaigning experience and the determination – some would say the lack of personal shame – to exploit his hold on the parliamentary seat to the full. Even when Labour ploughed what seemed like endless resources into the seat and had more than 500 volunteers knocking on doors on election day, Barwell was able to get more voters to the polling station than Labour, more supporters than had been seduced by the local Tory machine in thirty-six years.

No doubt our relationship would be back to normal in a few days.

Back to work

I woke up on Saturday morning and realised I had no campaigning to do. No hustings meeting. No ministerial visit. Not even a canvass session. It should have been liberating, but I felt lost.

That night, I had dinner with all my closest friends. It was my first proper night out in weeks and a chance to talk about what I had been through with those who know me best. I wanted to stay talking until the early hours, but exhaustion caught up with me.

And then on Monday it was back to work. I'd assumed there'd be a hung parliament and I'd get a protracted break while a new coalition agreement was hammered out. Against all the odds, however, we'd won outright and now David Cameron was forming the first majority Conservative government for eighteen years.

I was lucky enough to be offered a promotion to number three in the whips' office. This meant I'd be responsible for our operation in the chamber of the House of Commons, ensuring that ministers were well supported when they were at the Despatch Box, that votes came when planned and, most importantly of all, that we won those votes. Although I had some reservations about still not being able to speak in the Chamber – Labour had used this against me in the election to some effect – to be asked to be part of the government of this country is a tremendous honour and there's only one answer. Plus this was clearly an important role. The new government had a working majority of only sixteen, so votes were going to be much tighter in this parliament than they had been in the last.

The job came with a bizarre title, Comptroller of Her Majesty's Household, which sounded pretty grand. As well as my formal role as a whip, I had responsibilities at the State Opening of Parliament, royal garden parties and diplomatic receptions. I had an audience with Her Majesty at which she gave me my very own wand of office. Eat your heart out, Harry Potter.

The former and new officers of the royal household complete with wands

Wizarding aside, it was straight to work. There were lots of new faces in the whips' office who needed training up and we had an induction process to run for seventy-four new MPs.

I asked Mel Stride, who now sat next to me in the new whips' office, how his campaign had gone in Central Devon. He was rather bashful about it, but eventually confessed that his majority had increased from 9,230 to 21,265. It was a reminder that in politics what matters is not just how many votes you get, but how the other votes divide among your opponents. Nearly 23,000 people had voted for me; about 28,500 had voted for Mel. In Croydon Central, however, most of those who had not voted for me had backed Labour. In Mel's seat, the opposition vote had split almost equally between UKIP, Labour, the Liberal Democrats and the Greens. Some people have all the luck.

MPs from all parties stopped me in the corridors to congratulate me on making it back. The only exception was my former colleague in the whips' office Mark Lancaster, who was now a minister at the Ministry of Defence. With his usual dry sense of humour, he gave me a pat on the back and said, 'See? You're still here. What was all the fuss about?'

Praise from the PM

On Wednesday, the Prime Minister addressed the parliamentary party. It was a special occasion – Committee Room 14, where we traditionally meet, was packed to the rafters.

I was worried that our surprise victory might lead to a bout of triumphalism, a belief that we were back as the natural party of government when in fact we had only got 37 per cent of the vote. There was not a trace of that in the Prime Minister's speech, however. Quite the opposite: he was focused on what we needed to do to make sure we won again in 2020 – changing perceptions of the Conservative Party so that working people throughout the country see us, not Labour, as the party that shares their values.

During his speech, he mentioned some of the great individual results: Craig Mackinlay defeating Nigel Farage, Andrea Jenkyns beating Ed Balls, Tania Mathias beating Vince Cable, Byron Davies becoming the first Conservative to win Gower in south Wales for more than a century. At the end of the list, he mentioned my result. I was both touched and a little embarrassed. I'd done well to hold on given the other results in outer London, but at the end of the day I had turned a majority of nearly 3,000 into a majority of 165. It was hardly the stuff of political folklore – there were plenty of other people in the room who had done much better.

On the other hand, when the Prime Minister of your country pays you a compliment in front of your friends and peers, you just smile and accept it. I smiled and accepted it.

Epilogue

THERE ARE VERY few silver linings to representing an ultra-marginal seat, but one is that the people who voted for you can see that their vote counted. Over the following weeks, strangers would approach me in the street and say, 'I'm one of the 165.' I resisted the urge to give them a hug...

We had a huge thank-you party for everyone who worked on the campaign. Lots of people were keen to tell me about the part they had played – how they'd convinced a family of four to vote for me on polling day, or got two Conservative supporters who had just moved into the area to put themselves onto the electoral register back in February. Everyone could see that all their hard work had made the difference. The hours pounding the streets had been worth it.

Time passed. I struggled on at work, desperate to get to the summer recess and have a rest. Maybe if I wasn't so tired, I'd feel happier. I'd achieved my goal, kept the job I love. After five years of gruelling hard work, however, my majority had gone down, not up. How was I meant to feel about that? I needed some way to achieve closure.

An idea slowly began to take shape in my mind: rather than spending the summer recuperating, I would write a book about what I'd been through. Maybe it would prove cathartic.

It's certainly given me a chance to reflect on what we achieved. I made plenty of mistakes along the way, but overall I'm very proud of my work as the Member of Parliament for Croydon Central and of the campaign I ran. If the choice on the ballot paper had been between the political parties, Labour would have gained Croydon Central. With the help of hundreds of volunteers, I kept it in the Conservative column and that's no mean feat.

Would I like to have won by more? Of course, but Croydon Central is never going to be a safe Conservative seat. And if it's a choice between representing a safe seat or the place I grew up, it's Croydon every time.

Anyhow, I don't have time to dwell on the last election anymore. I've got a majority of 165 to defend in just over four years' time. Enough navel-gazing. Time to get back to work.

Appendix

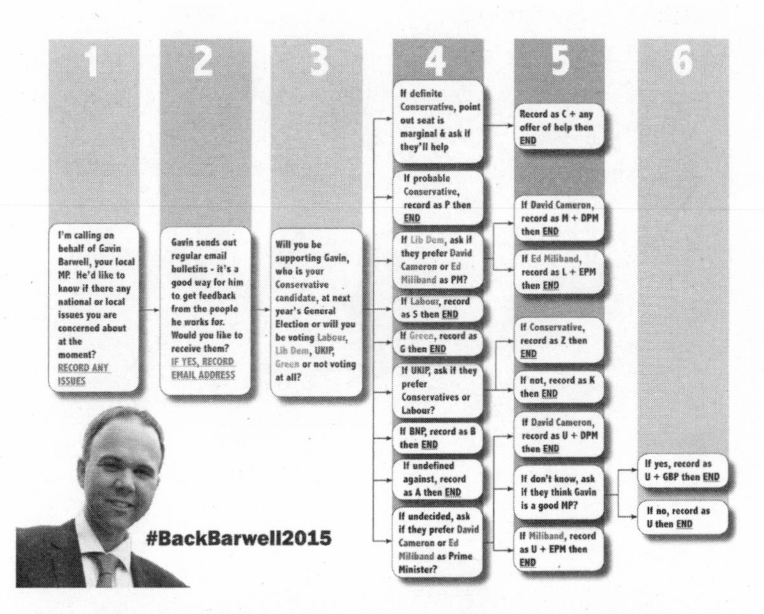

A flowchart showing the canvassing system we employed.

GAVIN BARWELL

A strong voice for Croydon

GAVIN HAS BEEN OUR MP SINCE 2010. HERE'S JUST A FEW OF THE THINGS HE'S DONE FOR CROYDON.

Helped bring Westfield and Hammerson to Croydon

Westfield and Hammerson's investment is the best news Croydon's had in years.

Westfield and Hammerson are investing over £1 billion in Croydon town centre. This will create thousands of jobs and encourage others to invest here too. Gavin played an important role in making it happen. Now he's working on getting investment for Portland Road and Central Parade, New Addington.

Changed the law to help those with mental health conditions

Gavin was the driving force behind ending legal discrimination against people with mental health conditions. He hopes that over time this will reduce the stigma surrounding mental health.

"Mr Barwell...deserves great credit for sponsoring this legislation. If, in his parliamentary career, he does nothing else of note, he can still reflect with pride on this achievement.

(THE TIMES 11th February 2013)

Helped toughen the law on drug driving

Taking Lillian's family to meet the Prime Minister

Gavin helped convince the Government to introduce Lillian's Law in memory of Lillian Groves, who was killed outside her home in New Addington by a driver who had taken drugs.

"We will be legislating properly for drug-related driving. It is right that it is put on to the statue book in the same way as drink driving and it would not be happening were it not for the very strong campaign Gavin Barwell has fought"

(David Cameron, 9th May 2012)

Won more funding for schools

Quest Academy pupils showing Gavin their new building.

Gavin has secured nearly £15 million from the Government to redevelop Quest Academy and almost £150 million to help Croydon Council create new school places to cope with our rising population.

And he helped persuade the Government to change the way it funds schools. As a result, Croydon schools will get £12 million more every year.

At New Addington's Pop-in Centre.

Put what's right for Croydon before politics

Gavin criticised the Conservative Council when he thought they'd made a mistake - for example, when they proposed extending parking restrictions and when they proposed cutting funding to New Addington's Pop-in Centre. Now he'll work constructively with the new Labour council.

Spoke up for us after the riots

Gavin has worked with Boris and Croydon Council to help Croydon recover from the riots.

Gavin pushed for tough sentences for those responsible. And he secured £25 million from the Government and the Mayor of London to rebuild our town's economy.

"Mr Barwell...impressed many in Westminster with his response to the devastating impact of last summer's riots on Croydon. At a time of crisis, he spoke out eloquently on behalf of the silent majority of law-abiding people in his town. We could do with a few more MPs like Mr Barwell in Westminster"

(Sun 28th May 2012)

GAVIN BARWELL - *A strong voice for Croydon* Conservatives

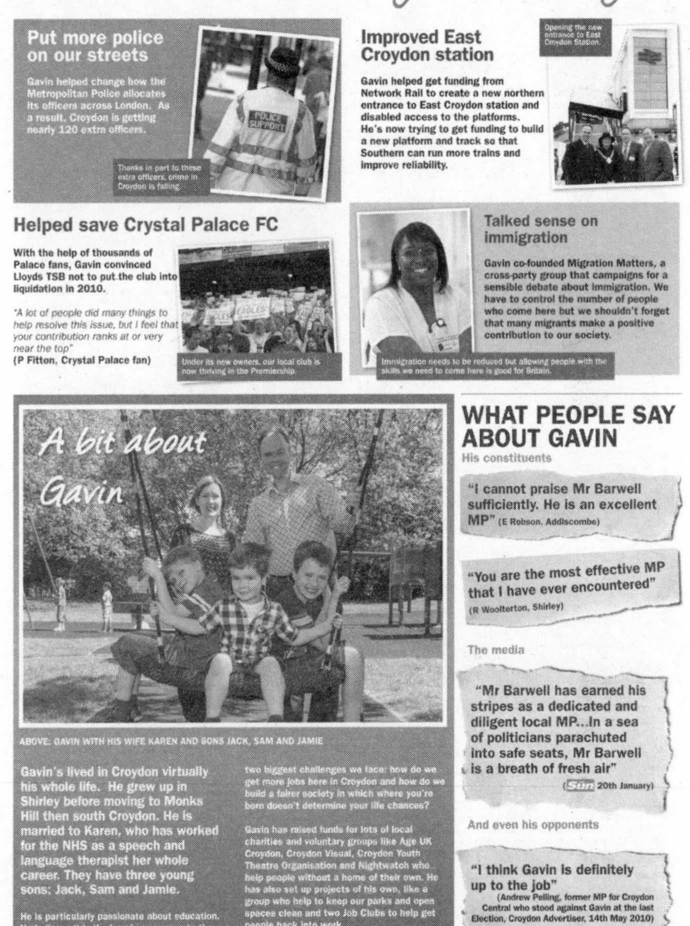

GAVIN BARWELL - A strong voice for Croydon

Put more police on our streets

Gavin helped change how the Metropolitan Police allocates its officers across London. As a result, Croydon is getting nearly 120 extra officers.

Thanks in part to these extra officers, crime in Croydon is falling.

Improved East Croydon station

Gavin helped get funding from Network Rail to create a new northern entrance to East Croydon station and disabled access to the platforms. He's now trying to get funding to build a new platform and track so that Southern can run more trains and improve reliability.

Opening the new entrance to East Croydon Station.

Helped save Crystal Palace FC

With the help of thousands of Palace fans, Gavin convinced Lloyds TSB not to put the club into liquidation in 2010.

"A lot of people did many things to help resolve this issue, but I feel that your contribution ranks at or very near the top"
(P Fitton, Crystal Palace fan)

Under its new owners, our local club is now thriving in the Premiership.

Talked sense on immigration

Gavin co-founded Migration Matters, a cross-party group that campaigns for a sensible debate about immigration. We have to control the number of people who come here but we shouldn't forget that many migrants make a positive contribution to our society.

Immigration needs to be reduced but allowing people with the skills we need to come here is good for Britain.

A bit about Gavin

ABOVE: GAVIN WITH HIS WIFE KAREN AND SONS JACK, SAM AND JAMIE

Gavin's lived in Croydon virtually his whole life. He grew up in Shirley before moving to Monks Hill then south Croydon. He is married to Karen, who has worked for the NHS as a speech and language therapist her whole career. They have three young sons: Jack, Sam and Jamie.

He is particularly passionate about education. He believes it is the long-term answer to the two biggest challenges we face: how do we get more jobs here in Croydon and how do we build a fairer society in which where you're born doesn't determine your life chances?

Gavin has raised funds for lots of local charities and voluntary groups like Age UK Croydon, Croydon Visual, Croydon Youth Theatre Organisation and Nightwatch who help people without a home of their own. He has also set up projects of his own, like a group who help to keep our parks and open spaces clean and two Job Clubs to help get people back into work.

WHAT PEOPLE SAY ABOUT GAVIN

His constituents

"I cannot praise Mr Barwell sufficiently. He is an excellent MP" (E Robson, Addiscombe)

"You are the most effective MP that I have ever encountered" (R Woolterton, Shirley)

The media

"Mr Barwell has earned his stripes as a dedicated and diligent local MP...In a sea of politicians parachuted into safe seats, Mr Barwell is a breath of fresh air" (Sun 20th January)

And even his opponents

"I think Gavin is definitely up to the job" (Andrew Pelling, former MP for Croydon Central who stood against Gavin at the last Election, Croydon Advertiser, 14th May 2010)

Keep in touch with Gavin's work for Croydon at www.gavinbarwell.com
@gavinbarwellmp www.facebook.com/gavin.barwell.mp

An A3 leaflet setting out my key achievements, which we delivered in an envelope along with a letter from Boris Johnson, inviting electors to my campaign launch.

GAVIN BARWELL
My plan for Croydon

Dear fellow resident,

Croydon could be one of the best places in the country to live. We're part of the greatest city in the world, yet on the edge of the beautiful North Downs countryside.

But we have our problems too - an unattractive town centre, insufficient infrastructure, inequality and a reputation problem that the 2011 riots made much worse. Things have started to improve recently, but there is still a lot to do.

This is a summary of my plan for how we make Croydon the place we all want it to be. You can read the whole plan at **www.gavinbarwell.com/vision**

I'd love to hear what you think of it - email me at gavin.barwell.mp@parliament.uk or write to 133 Wickham Road, Croydon CR0 8TE.

Gavin

Gavin Barwell
MP for Croydon Central

A strong economy that provides a job for everyone who wants one

To change Croydon for the better, we need a strong national economy. Labour gave us the worst recession since the 1930s and the biggest deficit in peace-time history. Under this Government, the UK is growing faster than any other advanced economy, the deficit is down and unemployment is falling faster than ever before (it's down nearly 40% in Croydon).

Westfield and Hammerson's investment won't just transform our shopping centre, it will encourage others to invest here

But I want everyone in our town to benefit from the recovery. For that to happen, we need to:

- stick to the plan that is working nationally;
- deliver the Westfield/Hammerson redevelopment of the Whitgift Centre as quickly as possible;
- transform the environment in the town centre so that people are more likely to visit and invest here;
- offer small and medium sized businesses tax incentives to relocate here; and
- regenerate our district centres like Central Parade and Portland Road.

If we do that, we can achieve the dream of full employment – a job for everyone who wants one. And we should increase the minimum wage so that everyone gets a fair reward for their hard work.

A decent education for all our children

Five years ago, Ashburton was a failing school. Conservatives closed it in the face of Labour opposition and today its replacement Oasis Academy Shirley Park is rated as outstanding.

I want all children in Croydon to go to a great school so that where you are born doesn't determine your chances in life.

Conservative councillors closed low-performing schools and replaced them with new academies. As a result, Croydon schools are now better than the national average and improving more quickly. But some are still not good enough.

I'd like to see parents have a wider choice of schools. In particular, it would be great to have a grammar school in Croydon.

And it would also be great to have a university campus in the town centre, making it cheaper for local people to study for a degree.

Immigration can be good for Britain, but overall numbers must be controlled

Controlled immigration

Allowing hard-working people with the skills we need to settle here is good for Britain. But we're a small, densely-populated country so there needs to be a limit on overall numbers - and allowing low-skilled people to settle here makes little sense.

This Government has reduced immigration by more than a quarter, but at the moment we don't have control of who comes here from Europe.

We need to change our relationship with the EU so we can reduce these numbers.

A zero-tolerance approach to crime

Crime in Croydon is falling, but it is still too high

Croydon's getting safer. There were 3,000 fewer crimes in the year to March 2014 than in the previous 12 months. But it's still too high in certain areas.

I'm particularly concerned about violent crime, including domestic violence, which is going up. I also want to see changes to the way the police use their stop and search powers. In the past, far too many innocent people from black and minority ethnic communities have been stopped.

I will always take a zero tolerance approach to crime – unlike my Labour opponent who, commenting on the recent fatal illegal rave at the Royal Mail building next to East Croydon station, said "youth is about exploration, pushing boundaries, seeking out fun and moulding your personality".

GAVIN BARWELL - *My Plan for Croydon* Conservatives

GAVIN BARWELL — My Plan for Croydon

Better healthcare

The NHS saved my life when I had cancer as a child. It is one of the best things about this country.

Some people get good care at Croydon University Hospital (CUH - or Mayday as many still think of it). But the recent inspection identified areas where care needs to improve. There's a strong case for making changes at other hospitals in south west London so we get more senior doctor cover at CUH 24 hours a day seven days a week.

We urgently need a new, larger A&E Department at Croydon University Hospital

One issue I am particularly passionate about is mental health. I introduced a law to try to reduce the stigma associated with mental illness, which often stops people seeking help. I will fight to ensure mental health services in Croydon get the priority they deserve.

Affordable housing

Labour talk about affordable housing, but they mean council and housing association homes. What people want is homes they can afford to buy.

We need more homes, but we mustn't concrete over precious green spaces. Building in the town centre is the answer

We have to face up to the fact that we need to build more homes - otherwise, prices will keep rising and home ownership will go back to being something for the privileged few. But we need to build them in the right places – principally the town centre – not on our precious green spaces.

Building more homes will also help to keep rents down in the private sector. I will oppose Labour's silly plan to impose a £200 per property tax on all private landlords, which will just get passed on to tenants.

We also need to build more council homes. And we should stop giving them to people who have only lived in Croydon for a year.

Enhanced infrastructure to support our growing population

People oppose building more homes because they worry our infrastructure couldn't cope. The answer is to improve our infrastructure. I will work to deliver:

- improvements to the A23, Croydon's key link to the motorway network;
- extra capacity on rail services to central London;
- an expanded ticket hall at East Croydon station and a link from Cherry Orchard Road to the new northern entrance of the station;
- increased capacity on and extensions to our tram system;
- funding for more school places (we're already getting eight times what we got from the last Government); and
- a new larger A&E Department at Croydon University Hospital.

We need longer and more frequent trains to tackle overcrowding

Fair funding for our public services

Historically, a number of the systems used to distribute funding for different public services have been unfair to Croydon. Working with others, I've managed to get the police and schools systems changed. As a result, we're getting 117 extra officers and our schools will get about £12 million more next April.

Croydon is getting an extra 117 police officers

Now we need to change the systems used to distribute the NHS budget and funding for local councils.

Our pensioners have worked hard for this country – we need to look after them in their retirement

A fairer society

I will set up a mentoring scheme for bright children from families where no-one has gone to university before, in order to help them achieve their potential.

I will oppose Labour's plans to give some out-of-work families more in benefits than the average working family earns.

And I will fight to protect key pensioner benefits like the Freedom Pass.

We need to renovate the Fairfield Halls so it can put on a much wider range of events

A richer cultural life

One of the things that would make Croydon a better place to live, as well as attracting people to invest here, is a richer cultural life. I will support:

- the renovation of the Fairfield Halls so that it can put on a much wider range of events;
- new leisure centres in New Addington and the town centre; and
- improved facilities at Lloyd Park so that it compares with somewhere like Battersea Park or the new Queen Elizabeth II park.

A cleaner environment

Why did our Labour Council not prosecute the group of travellers who dumped this rubbish?

Labour were right to focus on the state of our streets and open spaces in the recent local election campaign. But they've been running the Council for over 100 days now and things are no better. The answer is to catch the people responsible and punish them, rather than just cleaning up after them, as well as making sure everyone has access to and uses a wheelie bin and recycling boxes.

And we need to reduce air pollution, encouraging people to get out of their cars by making it safer to cycle.

Keep in touch with Gavin's work for Croydon at www.gavinbarwell.com
@gavinbarwellmp www.facebook.com/gavin.barwell.mp

An A3 leaflet that we delivered shortly after the campaign launch, which sets out some of the key pledges from our local manifesto, 'A Vision for Croydon'.

GAVIN BARWELL

Ideas to change Britain for the better

My last leaflet set out my vision for Croydon. This one sets out some of the things the Conservative Party will do if we win the next election - things we haven't been able to do over the last five years either because the country couldn't afford it or because we couldn't convince the Liberal Democrats to vote for them.

Let you keep more of the money you work hard to earn

When Labour left office in 2010, the personal allowance (the amount of money you can earn before you have to start paying income tax) was just £6,475.

By next April, we'll have increased that to £10,500. As a result, millions of us will have had our income tax bill cut by over £800 a year.

If we win next year's election, we'll increase it even more to £12,500. That will cut our tax bills by up to another £400 a year. And it'll mean that someone working full-time for the minimum wage won't pay any income tax at all.

We'll also increase the amount you have to earn before you start paying the 40p rate from £41,900 to £50,000. Only rich people were supposed to pay the 40p rate, but in recent years many middle-income people have been dragged in to it. That's not fair.

A Conservative Government will cut your income tax bill

As Conservatives, we believe people should keep more of the money they work hard to earn. So there's a clear choice at the next election: higher taxes under Labour, lower taxes under the Conservatives.

Increase the NHS budget every year

I'm passionate about our NHS. It saved my life when I had cancer as a child. And my wife and I don't have private health insurance, so if we or our children get sick it's the NHS we depend on.

This Government has increased the NHS budget every year, protecting it from the cuts we've had to make in other places. That money has paid for 6,500 more doctors, 3,300 more nurses and a Cancer Drugs Fund to make sure people get new, life-saving medicines.

If we win the next election, we'll keep increasing the NHS budget by more than the rate of inflation every year. But that's only possible because we've got our economy back on track. You can only have a well-funded NHS if you have a strong economy.

We will increase the NHS budget every year

Help young people get on the housing ladder

One of the most common concerns that people share with me is whether their children will ever be able to get on the property ladder in Croydon. We're in danger of going back to the days when owning your own home was only for a privileged few.

The key to keeping prices affordable is to build enough homes, but the Government also needs to help people get on the housing ladder.

We've already introduced the Help to Buy scheme that stops banks asking for massive deposits. But if we win the next election we'll take it further. We'll build 100,000 new starter homes. The only people that'll be able to buy them will be first-time buyers under the age of 40 and they'll cost 20% less than the normal market price.

Labour want more and more people to depend on the Council for housing. Their councillors are saying that at least 30% of all homes built in Croydon must be council or housing association homes. We want to help people fulfil their dream of owning their own home.

We want to help people fulfil their dream of owning their own home

GAVIN BARWELL - *A Strong Voice for Croydon* Conservatives

GAVIN BARWELL *Ideas to change Britain for the better*

4 Reduce immigration from the EU

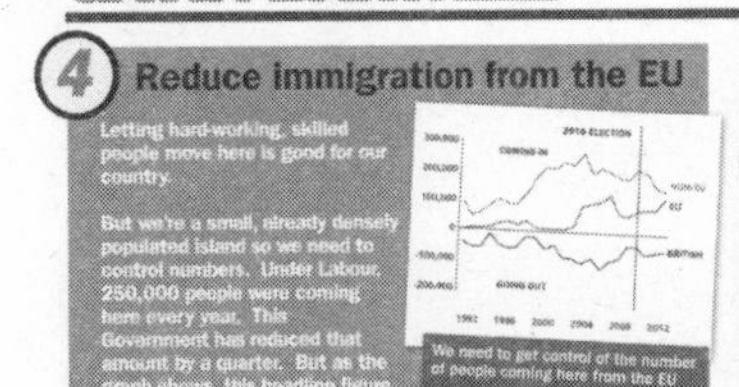

We need to get control of the number of people coming here from the EU

Letting hard-working, skilled people move here is good for our country.

But we're a small, already densely populated island so we need to control numbers. Under Labour, 250,000 people were coming here every year. This Government has reduced that amount by a quarter. But as the graph shows, this headline figure disguises the fact that while we have reduced immigration from outside the EU, immigration from inside the EU - over which we currently have no control - has increased.

We need to get back control of our borders. A Conservative Government will renegotiate our relationship with the EU. Changing the rules about freedom of movement is our main goal. You might doubt whether David Cameron can do this. But he's made it clear that he'll put the results of this renegotiation to a referendum. If you're not happy with the deal we're offered, you'll have the chance to vote to leave the EU. We're the only party offering you that choice.

6 Let people pass on their pension tax-free when they die

As well as helping young people, we want our elderly people to enjoy their retirement with dignity and security. That's why we've:

You should be able to pass your pension to a loved one when you die without the Government taxing it

- **protected pensioner benefits like the Winter Fuel Allowance and the Freedom Pass;**
- **made sure the basic state pension increases in line with whichever is higher of price inflation, wage inflation or 2.5% (so we don't repeat the 75p a week increase pensioners got under the last Government); and**
- **scrapped compulsory annuities, giving people freedom to spend the money they've saved however they like.**

But at the moment when someone dies, the Government taxes the pension they've saved at 55 per cent before it goes to their loved ones. We'll scrap that tax completely.

5 End long-term youth unemployment

Young people should be earning or learning, not on the dole

One of this Government's successes is the massive drop in unemployment. In my constituency, it's down 41% since the last election. And youth unemployment is down 45%. These aren't just statistics - over 1,200 of the people I represent have found a job and can now provide for themselves and their families.

But if we win the election, we want to end long-term youth unemployment altogether. We're focusing on young people because all the evidence shows that if they're out of work for the first few years after they leave education, it has a big impact on the rest of their lives. They should be earning or learning, not on the dole.

So if 18-21 year olds who don't have children and are fit to work haven't found a job in six months, they'll have to choose between taking an apprenticeship or a Community Work Placement - 10 hours of looking for a job and 30 hours of useful work a week (things like making meals for older people, cleaning up litter or working for local charities). To make sure they have that choice, we'll fund three million apprenticeships that combine training with work experience and a wage.

We know that'll cost a lot of money. So we'll:

- reduce the cap on the total amount of benefits an out-of-work family can get from £26,000 to £23,000 a year (under the last Labour Government, some families were getting over £50,000 a year); and
- stop unemployed 18-21 year olds from claiming Housing Benefit so they can leave home (but we'll still help people like care-leavers who need their own home).

As Conservatives, we believe it's unfair for people who aren't working to be better off than working people. And we'd rather spend taxpayers' money helping people into work.

7 Be able to see a GP seven days a week

Another complaint I hear a lot is about how difficult it is to get an appointment with a GP. This is just one consequence of the last Government's failure to provide the extra infrastructure our growing population needs.

We want everyone to be able to see a GP seven days a week

The first and most obvious thing we need to do is recruit more GPs. Our aim is to make sure the NHS has nearly 5,000 more by 2020.

But we also need to change primary care to fit in with the fact that many of us lead much busier lives. By 2020, we want everyone to be able to see a GP seven days a week - and to have email, Skype or phone consultations rather than face-to-face appointments when it's safe to do so and that's what patients want. We'd also like to see smarter use of electronic prescriptions and booking appointments online.

8 Scrap the Human Rights Act

Labour's Human Rights Act meant it took years to deport Abu Qatada

Basic rights like the right to free speech and the right to practice your religion are fundamental pillars of a free society. But in recent years the way the European Court of Human Rights has interpreted those rights has become more and more bizarre. It's stopped us deporting suspected terrorists and told our Parliament that it must change the law to give convicted criminals the right to vote - even though the majority of people don't agree with this.

That's why a future Conservative Government will scrap Labour's Human Rights Act and pass a new British Bill of Rights so that British judges make decisions about our human rights in British courts.

Keep in touch with Gavin's work for Croydon at www.gavinbarwell.com
@gavinbarwellmp www.facebook.com/gavin.barwell.mp ☎ 020 8663 8741

An A3 leaflet that we delivered shortly after the 2014 Conservative Party conference, which sets out some of the key announcements made at the conference.

OFFICE OF GAVIN BARWELL MP
Member of Parliament for Croydon Central
133 Wickham Road, Croydon, CR0 8TE

March 2015

Dear fellow resident,

I got involved in politics because I'm passionate about building a fairer society.

I want all children to go to a great school like I was lucky enough to do. Where you happen to grow up shouldn't determine your chances in life. That's why I've fought for extra funding for schools in deprived areas. That's why I've supported the closure of schools like Ashburton and Selsdon High that were failing our children. And that's why I value teachers so highly.

I want enough jobs for everyone who needs one. Being out of work doesn't just leave people hard up; it affects their sense of self-worth and even their health. I'm a Conservative because over the years Conservative policies have been shown to create more jobs. Unemployment here in Croydon Central has halved over the last five years. Labour mean well, but every single time they've been in government unemployment has gone up.

I believe in fair pay. We can't all be Premiership footballers or popstars; most of us have to do jobs that are much less glamorous and don't pay anything like as well. Conservatives were wrong to oppose a minimum wage back in the 1990s. I'm proud that this Government has increased it and I want to see further increases so that everyone benefits from the recovery.

I believe in making sure the wealthy pay their fair share in tax. Under Labour, hedge fund managers paid a lower rate than the people they employed to clean their offices. This Government has put a stop to that. It's reformed Stamp Duty so that most people pay less but those buying the most expensive properties pay more. And it's cracking down on tax evasion.

I believe in equality. That's why I've supported equal pay; campaigned against the abuse of stop and search; spoken out against Islamophobia at home and the persecution of Christians abroad; introduced a law to reduce the stigma attached to mental ill health; and voted for same sex marriage. People should be judged by their actions, not their gender, skin colour, faith, disability or who they love.

US President Obama says, 'Great Britain and the United States are two economies that are standing out at a time when a lot of other countries are having problems, so we must be doing something right'

I believe people who work hard should be better off as a result. That's why I support low rates of income tax. And it's why I support a cap on the amount of benefits an out-of-work family can receive. Under Labour, some families were receiving more than £50,000 a year. Now no-one can get more than the average family earns.

You may normally support Labour, but if you're unsure about Ed Miliband and whether he can be trusted with our economy, I hope you feel that our politics are not so different and might consider lending me your vote this time. Thank you for taking the time to read this letter.

Gavin

Gavin Barwell
Member of Parliament for Croydon Central

PS If you're undecided about how to vote and would like to talk to me in person, email gavin@backbarwell.com or call 020 8660 0491.

MY PLAN FOR CROYDON

A strong economy that provides a job for everyone who wants one

- Deliver the Westfield/Hammerson redevelopment of the Whitgift Centre as quickly as possible.
- Encourage businesses to locate here by transforming the environment in the town centre and offering tax incentives to small and medium sized firms.
- Regenerate our district centres like Central Parade and Portland Road.

A decent education for all our children

- Raise standards in our schools so that as a minimum every child - apart from those with a significant learning difficulty - leaves school with a decent pass in Maths and English.
- Give parents a wider choice of schools - hopefully including a grammar school.
- Work to open a campus of Roehampton University in Croydon.

A zero-tolerance approach to crime

- Give more priority to tackling violent crime including sexual violence.
- Reform stop and search to increase community confidence in the police.

Better healthcare

- Raise standards at Croydon University Hospital.
- Ensure mental health is given the priority it deserves.

Affordable housing

- Build more homes, but in the right places - not on our precious green spaces.
- Oppose Labour's plan to make private landlords pay an annual tax on every home they rent out - it will just get passed on to already hard-pressed tenants.

Enhanced infrastructure to support our growing population

- Improve the A23, Croydon's key link to the motorway network, at Fiveways and Purley Cross.
- Increase capacity and improve reliability on rail services to London Bridge and Victoria and improve key stations like East Croydon.
- Increase capacity on and extend our tram system.
- Secure funding from the Government to help Croydon Council provide sufficient school places and for a new larger A&E Department at Croydon University Hospital.

A cleaner environment

- Make sure every household has access to a bin and recycling facilities and then start to penalise those who won't recycle.
- Prosecute those who flytip, rather than just cleaning up after them.
- Encourage more people to cycle by making our roads more cyclist friendly.

A richer cultural life

- Renovate the Fairfield Halls so that it can put on a wider range of shows.
- Refurbish New Addington leisure centre and build a new leisure centre in the town centre.
- Improve facilities at one of our major parks so that it compares with somewhere like Battersea Park or the new Queen Elizabeth II Park.

A direct mail campaign to wavering Labour supporters.

OFFICE OF GAVIN BARWELL MP
Member of Parliament for Croydon Central
133 Wickham Road, Croydon, CR0 8TE

March 2015

Dear fellow resident,

Croydon is one of the most diverse parts of the country. It's one of the things I love about it. Over the last five years, I've tried to represent the concerns of all the communities who call our town home.

I've opposed the abuse of stop and search (official figures show people from black and ethnic minority communities are six times more likely to be stopped). When I was growing up the Conservative Party didn't want to know about institutional racism within the police, ignoring the overwhelming case for an inquiry into the murder of Stephen Lawrence. I'm proud that this Government is addressing this issue. The number of stops has fallen from 1.5 million a year under Labour to a million a year today, but there's more to do.

I helped convince the Chancellor to reform Air Passenger Duty. The banded system introduced by Labour unfairly penalised many of my constituents with families in the Caribbean or south Asia.

I've spoken out against the rising tide of Islamophobia, working closely with South Norwood Islamic Community Centre, **and also against the persecution of Christians abroad.**

I've pressed the police to devote more resources to catching and prosecuting burglars who are targeting the homes of south Asian families.

I've campaigned for an independent investigation into alleged war crimes in Sri Lanka on behalf of my Tamil constituents, many of whom still don't know the fate of loved ones.

And I co-founded a cross-party group, Migration Matters, to promote the benefits of immigration. We're a small country so there's a limit to the number of people we can let in every year, but too often discussion of this issue in the media overlooks the huge contribution migrants have made to our economy, public services and society as a whole.

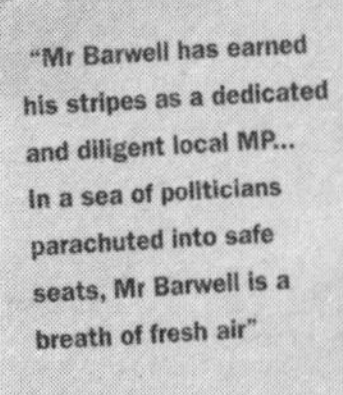

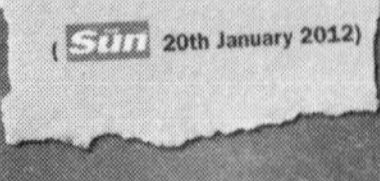

You may never have voted Conservative before, but if you share my values - the importance of family, the value of education, reward for hard work - and you think I have been a good MP, I hope you will lend me your vote on 7th May. At a time when UKIP are demonising immigrants and threatening to abolish the laws that prevent employers from racially discriminating, your vote could make all the difference.

Thanks for taking the time to read this letter,

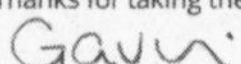

Gavin Barwell
Member of Parliament for Croydon Central

PS If you're undecided about how to vote and would like to talk to me in person, email **gavin@backbarwell.com** or call 020 8660 0491.

MY PLAN FOR CROYDON

A strong economy that provides a job for everyone who wants one

- Deliver the Westfield/Hammerson redevelopment of the Whitgift Centre as quickly as possible.
- Encourage businesses to locate here by transforming the environment in the town centre and offering tax incentives to small and medium sized firms.
- Regenerate our district centres like Central Parade and Portland Road.

A decent education for all our children

- Raise standards in our schools so that as a minimum every child - apart from those with a significant learning difficulty - leaves school with a decent pass in Maths and English.
- Give parents a wider choice of schools - hopefully including a grammar school.
- Work to open a campus of Roehampton University in Croydon.

A zero-tolerance approach to crime

- Give more priority to tackling violent crime including sexual violence.
- Reform stop and search to increase community confidence in the police.

Better healthcare

- Raise standards at Croydon University Hospital.
- Ensure mental health is given the priority it deserves.

Affordable housing

- Build more homes, but in the right places - not on our precious green spaces.
- Oppose Labour's plan to make private landlords pay an annual tax on every home they rent out - it will just get passed on to already hard-pressed tenants.

Enhanced infrastructure to support our growing population

- Improve the A23, Croydon's key link to the motorway network, at Fiveways and Purley Cross.
- Increase capacity and improve reliability on rail services to London Bridge and Victoria and improve key stations like East Croydon.
- Increase capacity on and extend our tram system.
- Secure funding from the Government to help Croydon Council provide sufficient school places and for a new larger A&E Department at Croydon University Hospital.

US President Obama says, 'Great Britain and the United States are two economies that are standing out at a time when a lot of other countries are having problems, so we must be doing something right'

A cleaner environment

- Make sure every household has access to a bin and recycling facilities and then start to penalise those who won't recycle.
- Prosecute those who flytip, rather than just cleaning up after them.
- Encourage more people to cycle by making our roads more cyclist friendly.

A richer cultural life

- Renovate the Fairfield Halls so that it can put on a wider range of shows.
- Refurbish New Addington leisure centre and build a new leisure centre in the town centre.
- Improve facilities at one of our major parks so that it compares with somewhere like Battersea Park or the new Queen Elizabeth II Park.

Want to learn more about why Gavin is so passionate about representing his home town in Parliament? Scan this code to watch a short video on your smartphone

A direct mail campaign to electors from black and ethnic minority communities.

OFFICE OF GAVIN BARWELL MP
Member of Parliament for Croydon Central
133 Wickham Road, Croydon, CR0 8TE

March 2015

Dear fellow resident,

On 7th May you'll have the chance, for the first time in your life, to have a say in who runs our country. It's a big decision.

Representing my home town in Parliament for the last five years has been a huge honour. I've tried my best to do a good job for everyone who calls Croydon home, but particularly young people who many politicians overlook.

I've supported policies that encourage firms to employ young people. As a result, the number of young people in Croydon who are out of work is less than half what it was under Labour.

I've helped bring Westfield to Croydon. Their and Hammerson's redevelopment of the Whitgift Centre won't just transform Croydon town centre and help change our town's reputation, it will create thousands more jobs.

I've opposed the abuse of stop and search (Official figures show people from black and ethnic minority communities are six times more likely to be stopped). I'm proud that this Government is doing something about it, reducing the number of stops from 1.5 million a year under Labour to a million a year today, but there's more to do.

I've backed building more homes as well as extra help from first-time buyers so young people have a chance of getting on the housing ladder.

I'm working hard to improve our rail service to central London. Southern's current performance is unacceptable. We need a much more reliable service and longer, more frequent trains to tackle overcrowding.

And I've given nearly 200 local young people work experience in my office and a reference on their CV.

If you share my belief in freedom to live the life we choose and keep more of the money we work hard to earn and you think I have been a good local MP, please give me your support on 7th May. This is going to be the closest election in a generation. At a time when UKIP are demonising immigrants and threatening to abolish the laws that prevent employers from racially discriminating, your vote could make all the difference.

Thank you for taking the time to read this letter,

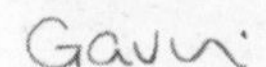

Gavin Barwell
Member of Parliament for Croydon Central

PS If you're undecided about how to vote and would like to talk to me in person - or you're going to vote for me and would like to get involved in my campaign - email **gavin@backbarwell.com** or call 020 8660 0491.

US President Obama says, 'Great Britain and the United States are two economies that are standing out at a time when a lot of other countries are having problems, so we must be doing something right'

WHY WE'RE BACKING BARWELL

"I was one of those young voters who was so angry at all politicians as I'd often say 'they're all the same.' But Gavin genuinely isn't the same as all the others and doesn't fit the stereotype of an MP, let alone a Conservative one: he is young, pretty funny and most surprisingly of all quite liberal! Not only is he a good MP, he is also a great person. Who wouldn't vote for a guy like that?" **Felicia Ajayi**

"When I left school in 2013, I chose not to go to university. It was a tough choice to make, especially as I found it very hard to get a job afterwards. However, Gavin understood this and I know he helped me and hundreds of others like me to get our foot in the door with his internships. It really gave me the experience and confidence to get the jobs I wanted and I can't thank him enough. Gavin really is an excellent MP who truly knows the issues young people face." **Matt O'Flynn**

"Gavin works tirelessly for young residents, be it speaking to students to demonstrate the importance of voting to fighting for starter homes to help young people on to the housing ladder. We need an MP like Gavin who is willing to put the needs of young people before politics." **Hollie Stacey**

"Gavin has been a great MP for Croydon Central and is the kind of person I want in Parliament: genuine, compassionate and open-minded. He always puts his constituents first and stands up for our town's diversity. I'm really pleased with his opposition to stop-and-search which unfairly targets black and Asian youth. He's passionate about the issues that concern young people the most: improved standards in schools, getting a decent job and buying a first home." **Samir Dwesar**

"I have never met someone who has done as much for Croydon as Gavin; he is always out in the area meeting people, listening to what they have to say and doing what he can to be their voice in government. Gavin also brought Westfield and Hammerson to Croydon. I personally can't wait to see our high street transformed. It's so important that young people vote for what matters to them, in my opinion it's got to be Gavin." **Amy Pollard**

A direct mail campaign to electors who were eligible to vote at their first general election.

OFFICE OF GAVIN BARWELL MP
Member of Parliament for Croydon Central
133 Wickham Road, Croydon, CR0 8TE

March 2015

Dear fellow resident,

This year's election is the most important in a generation

On 7th May, we have a choice. Stick with David Cameron and the economic plan that is delivering a record number of jobs, low inflation, a falling deficit and now rising wages.

Or put Ed Miliband in charge, possibly propped up by Alex Salmond, and go back to the higher spending, paid for by higher borrowing, that took us to the brink of bankruptcy in 2010. The stakes could not be higher.

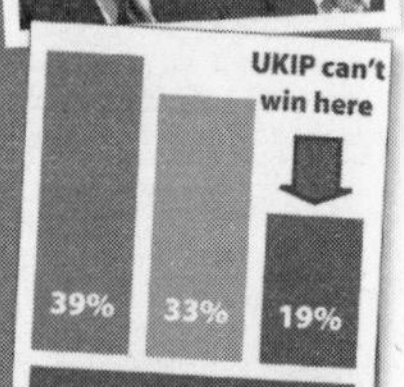

How you vote will also decide whether I continue as your local MP

I hope you feel you have an MP who is passionate about Croydon and works hard. I'm proud of what I have achieved - bringing Westfield here, getting money from the Government to rebuild after the riots, more funding for our schools and local hospital - but there's so much more to do. With your support, I'd love to continue.

Your vote could make the difference

In many parts of the country, the same party wins every time, but Croydon Central is one of the closely-fought constituencies that decide who runs the country. Your vote could make the difference between David Cameron or Ed Miliband getting the keys to Downing Street.

Vote UKIP, get Labour - and no EU referendum

A recent opinion poll showed that Croydon Central is a two-horse race between Labour and the Conservatives. UKIP can't win here - the bookies make them 100/1 outsiders.

If people who don't want Labour to win vote UKIP, they're not just wasting their votes; by splitting the anti-Labour vote, they're actually helping Labour win. That's what happened in last year's Croydon Council elections - UKIP didn't get a single councillor elected, but they took enough votes from the Conservatives for Labour to take control of the Council. Don't let it happen again. If you want to keep me as your local MP, you don't want Ed Miliband as PM and you want an EU referendum, you need to vote Conservative.

I don't just need your support, I need your help

Labour are pouring resources into this seat. If you want me to win, there are things you can do to help, some of which will only take a few moments - see over the page for details.

Thanks for taking the time to read this letter,

Gavin Barwell
Member of Parliament for Croydon Central

PS If you're undecided about how to vote and would like to talk to me in person, email gavin@backbarwell.com or call 020 8660 0491.

Croydon Central is a two-horse race between Labour and the Conservatives. If you don't want Ed Miliband as Prime Minister you need to vote for Gavin

"Based on current polling UKIP is going to cost Gavin his seat"

(Dr Matthew Goodwin, Associate Professor of Politics at Nottingham University)

HOW YOU CAN HELP KEEP GAVIN AS YOUR LOCAL MP AND STOP ED MILIBAND BECOMING PRIME MINISTER

1. Email gavin@backbarwell.com or call 020 8660 0491 to confirm that you will be voting Conservative - it will save us having to call on you during the election. If there are other Conservative supporters in your household, let us know about them too.

2. Put up the enclosed poster in your window. It'll stop other parties knocking on your door and help Gavin at the same time.

3. If there's any chance that you're going to be away or you'd just find it more convenient to vote by post on 7th May, complete the enclosed postal vote application form and send it to the Town Hall. If you need extra copies or you're going away well before 7th May (in which case a postal vote is no good - you'll need a proxy to vote for you), call 020 8660 0491.

4. Talk to your neighbours and friends who live in the area (Addington Village, Addiscombe, Forestdale, Monks Hill, New Addington, Park Hill, Shirley and Woodside). If they're undecided, a word from you may make the difference.

5. If you have a bit of spare time and could help by delivering a few of Gavin's leaflets in your area, calling on electors or reminding Conservative supporters to vote on polling day, email gavin@backbarwell.com or call 020 8660 0491.

6. If you can afford to make a donation to help fund Gavin's campaign, send a cheque made payable to Croydon Conservative Federation to 36 Brighton Road, Purley CR8 2LG.

7. If you'd be prepared to invite a few of your neighbours round to your house to meet Gavin, email gavin@backbarwell.com or call 020 8660 0491.

"I think Gavin is definitely up to the job"

(Andrew Pelling, former MP for Croydon Central who stood against Gavin at the last Election, Croydon Advertiser, 14th May 2010)

"Mr Barwell has earned his stripes as a dedicated and diligent local MP... In a sea of politicians parachuted into safe seats, Mr Barwell is a breath of fresh air"

(Sun 20th January 2012)

"You are the most effective MP that I have ever encountered"

(R Woolterton, Shirley)

A letter to potential supporters, which we distributed in March to communicate that Croydon Central was a marginal seat and to appeal for help with the campaign.

Local people are backing BARWELL

Local people are backing Gavin Barwell to continue as our MP. They value his track record over the last five years and back him to be the strong voice for Croydon that we need.

Gary and Natasha Groves
New Addington residents

"On the 26th June 2010 our lives were ripped apart when our 14 year-old daughter was hit by a drug driver outside our family home. Without the support and hard work from Gavin, we would not have been able to change the law to stop this from happening to someone else. For us Gavin is a miracle worker. We have no question as to where our vote will be going."

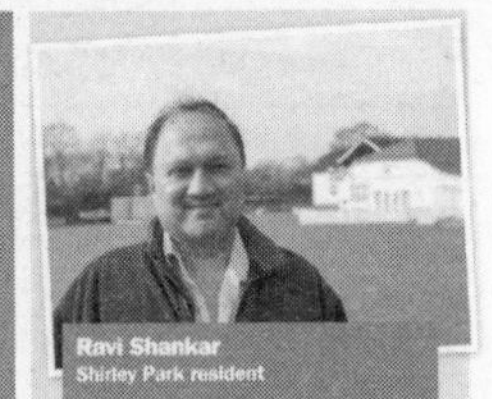

Ravi Shankar
Shirley Park resident

"Gavin works very hard for us all in Croydon. He's always approachable and understands what all the different communities need locally. It doesn't matter who you are or where you're from, Gavin is always there to help."

"I'm a mum with two young boys, my husband owns a small business. It's tough to make ends meet, but I know that the Conservatives are on our side. Recently my husband has been able to expand his business giving our little ones a more secure future."

Collette Bashford
Foresdale resident

See people's views on Gavin in their own words by scanning this barcode on your smart-phone, or go to
www.backbarwell.com/backingbarwell

Boris Johnson
Mayor of London

"Croydon needs Barwell. Gavin's worked with me to bring Westfield to the town, put 120 extra police officers on Croydon's streets and improve the tram system. We need more MPs like him."

"A lot of people have an understandably negative view of MPs, thinking that they're out of touch and only in it for themselves. I've worked with Gavin for nearly five years and he's not like that at all: he's down to earth, really knows what he's talking about and constantly fights for what's best for Croydon. I wouldn't want anyone else as my MP."

Katrina Jones
Woodside resident

For a hard-working, effective local MP who is a strong voice for Croydon, back Gavin Barwell on 7th May

Maureen Martin
Executive Head, Coloma Trust

"Coloma has been very well supported by Gavin since his election as our local MP. He has taken a personal interest in our students' successes and challenges and has greatly encouraged our work in transforming The Quest Academy – Coloma Trust to become the school of choice in its local area. Gavin consistently demonstrates his passion for all Croydon young people to receive the very best possible education. We are most grateful to him."

Gavin believes 100% in our young people

"I'm very happy with Gavin – you couldn't ask for a more committed and hardworking local MP. He grew up in Croydon and believes 100% in the area's vast potential – especially when it concerns our young people. He has worked hard to make Croydon's exciting regeneration plans happen and improve our transport links. He's got my vote."

Alan Bates
Central Croydon resident and East Croydon Station commuter

"At the last election I voted for Andrew Pelling, but Gavin gets my vote this time"

"At the last Election, I voted for Andrew Pelling. Gavin has proved an equally hard-working and effective local MP. He'll be getting my vote this time."

Shirley Trimmer
Shirley resident

David Harmes
Addiscombe resident and former residents' association chair

"I've had the good fortune to work with Gavin on a number of occasions over the years. He has great passion and a seemingly boundless energy to represent Croydon and get us the best deal he can, Addiscombe couldn't have a better MP - all the while being a family man too!"

"I have found Gavin to be one of the hardest working MPs that I have come across. He is passionate about representing all the different communities who've made Croydon their home and he can be relied on to help with problems of his constituents: he certainly did so for my family."

Mahmood Hassan
Shirley resident

"Gavin works for all our communities"

"Gavin lives and breathes Croydon"

"I served as a councillor for Ashburton for over 20 years and over that time worked with many MPs. Gavin's commitment to Croydon, and the people he represents, is beyond compare. He lives and breathes Croydon, working tirelessly for his constituents, no matter the issue."

Eddy Arram
Former Ashburton Councillor

Neelofar Khan
Croydon business owner

"The NHS saved Gavin's life"

"My main concern is the NHS. Gavin had cancer as a child and the NHS saved his life so I know he cares passionately about it. He's secured extra funding for the NHS locally and now he's campaigning for a new Accident & Emergency Department at our local hospital. I'd expect nothing less from our local MP."

www.backbarwell.com | 020 8660 0491 | gavin@backbarwell.com | facebook.com/backbarwell | twitter.com/backbarwell | Conservatives

A leaflet we delivered at the start of the short campaign, containing endorsements from people in different parts of the constituency.

Great news - new A&E for our hospital

Some people question Conservatives' commitment to the NHS.

They're wrong. My wife works for it, it saved my life when I had cancer as a child and it gave outstanding care to my Dad when he was dying of Alzheimer's. I couldn't be more committed to it.

Since I was elected as an MP, I've tried to pay back the debt I owe. I've supported increases in the NHS budget and now **I've secured over £20 million for a new Emergency Department** at our local hospital. This is what being a good local MP is all about - lobbying to get a better deal for our town.

The current Department is too small for our growing population. The new one will be much bigger with state-of-the-art facilities.

Building work will start in Autumn 2015

The NHS isn't perfect, but the principle - that if you get sick or hurt you don't have to worry whether you can afford treatment - is one of the best things about this country.

I will continue to do everything I can to defend and improve it.

A leaflet we delivered shortly after the government announced funding to build a new accident and emergency department at Croydon University Hospital.

Mr and Mrs G Groves
Headley Drive
New Addington
Croydon

April 2015

Dear neighbour,

Let me introduce ourselves. We are the parents of 4 children and have lived happily in New Addington all our lives. On the 26th June 2010 our lives were ripped apart when our 14 year old daughter was hit by an uninsured Drug Driver outside our family home. Many of you will have read about our story in the local newspapers and seen news reports following our continuing journey. We are the family of Lillian Groves.

Desperate for information and advice following a lengthy disappointing Court Case we sought help from Gavin Barwell our local MP. We first met Gavin in July 2011 at the Addington Community Centre during one of his constituent surgery clinics. For us as you can imagine this was a very difficult and emotional meeting.

Being a family man himself with 3 boys and newly elected as Croydon Central MP our story also affected Gavin and he was clearly moved by our loss but remained professional but sympathetic throughout our meeting, giving us his word that he would follow lines of enquiries that we had and feed back to us. He later became a vital piece in our journey towards our ongoing campaign 'Lillian's Law – Drugs Don't Drive'.

Whilst we began petitioning the streets of Croydon and New Addington Gavin was lobbying Lillian's Law at every opportunity in the House of Commons. In November 2011 Gavin had arranged for us to meet with the Prime Minister David Cameron and this proved to be a major step in the forthcoming new Law.

…e his main MP duties
…t. In June 2014 Gavin
…r Lillian's Law Trust Fund
… which was clearly spoken
… forwarded on by David

…t was an incredibly moving
…hen you see the way in
…gedy, then you could have
…ne young woman. I'm sure
…have done in her name."

…s is that without the
…e would not have happened.
… have found ourselves in
is that our local MP Gavin Barwell went above and beyond his duties to help a family set about change. A change for the better, a change for us all.

For us Gavin is a miracle worker and I would recommend him and his services to anyone who needs help, support and advice. I have no question as to where our vote will be going in this election.

Yours faithfully,

Natasha and Gary Groves

Promoted by Ian James Parker, on behalf of Gavin Barwell, both of 86 Brighton Road, Purley CR8 2LJ.
Printed by St Ives plc, The Old Dairy, Melcombe Road, Bath, Somerset, BA2 3LR.

An example of the handwritten-style endorsement letters we delivered during the short campaign. This one was delivered throughout New Addington, where Lillian's parents lived.

Not sure who to vote for?

MAY 7

Your vote on 7th May will help to decide who runs our country for the next five years and whether local man Gavin Barwell remains as our MP.

Who do you want as our MP?

It's a two-horse race between Gavin Barwell and Labour's Sarah Jones. Here are some of the key differences:

Track Records

Gavin Barwell has been our MP for the last five years and before that was a councillor for 12 years. He's achieved a lot including getting funding from the Government and Boris Johnson to rebuild after the riots, helping to bring Westfield to Croydon and convincing the Government to build a new Emergency Department at our local hospital.

Labour's **Sarah Jones** has no experience as an MP or local councillor.

On crime

Gavin believes in a zero tolerance approach to crime.

Sarah says Gavin is "too macho" when it comes to crime. Commenting on last year's illegal rave at the former Royal Mail sorting office next to East Croydon station, which resulted in serious injuries (from which one person sadly later died) and major criminal damage, she said "youth is about exploration, pushing boundaries, seeking out fun and moulding your personality".

On green spaces

Gavin says we should protect our remaining green spaces - new housing should go on brownfield sites.

Sarah believes the Council needs to "be brave and build in places people might not want us to"

On school fields

Gavin opposed Croydon Council's plans to build on some school playing fields.

Sarah refused to comment on Croydon Council's plans to build on some school playing fields for fear of upsetting her Labour colleagues.

On Rents

Gavin opposes Croydon Council's plan to impose a tax on all private landlords, which he argues will just get passed on to hard-pressed tenants.

Sarah supports Croydon Council's plans to impose a tax on all private landlords.

On our future

Gavin has published his vision for the future of Croydon - see www.gavinbarwell.com/visionforcroydon

Sarah hasn't published any manifesto.

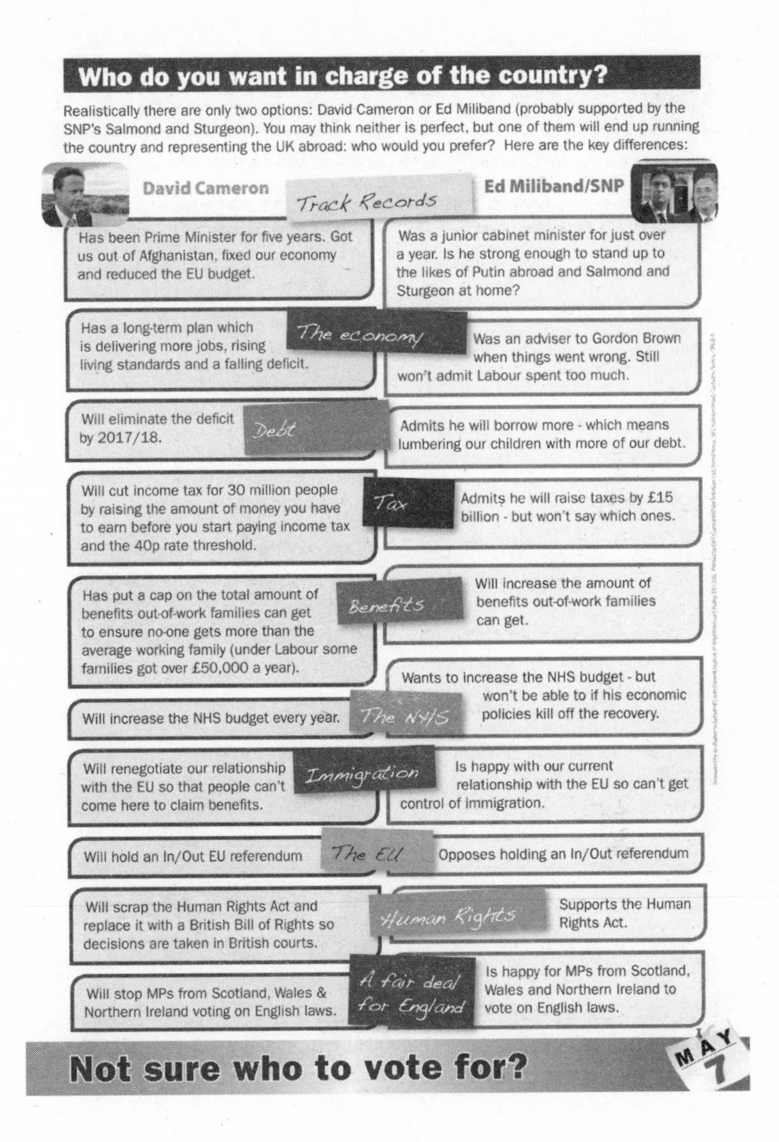

Who do you want in charge of the country?

Realistically there are only two options: David Cameron or Ed Miliband (probably supported by the SNP's Salmond and Sturgeon). You may think neither is perfect, but one of them will end up running the country and representing the UK abroad: who would you prefer? Here are the key differences:

	David Cameron	Ed Miliband/SNP
Track Records	Has been Prime Minister for five years. Got us out of Afghanistan, fixed our economy and reduced the EU budget.	Was a junior cabinet minister for just over a year. Is he strong enough to stand up to the likes of Putin abroad and Salmond and Sturgeon at home?
The economy	Has a long-term plan which is delivering more jobs, rising living standards and a falling deficit.	Was an adviser to Gordon Brown when things went wrong. Still won't admit Labour spent too much.
Debt	Will eliminate the deficit by 2017/18.	Admits he will borrow more - which means lumbering our children with more of our debt.
Tax	Will cut income tax for 30 million people by raising the amount of money you have to earn before you start paying income tax and the 40p rate threshold.	Admits he will raise taxes by £15 billion - but won't say which ones.
Benefits	Has put a cap on the total amount of benefits out-of-work families can get to ensure no-one gets more than the average working family (under Labour some families got over £50,000 a year).	Will increase the amount of benefits out-of-work families can get.
The NHS	Will increase the NHS budget every year.	Wants to increase the NHS budget - but won't be able to if his economic policies kill off the recovery.
Immigration	Will renegotiate our relationship with the EU so that people can't come here to claim benefits.	Is happy with our current relationship with the EU so can't get control of immigration.
The EU	Will hold an In/Out EU referendum	Opposes holding an In/Out referendum
Human Rights	Will scrap the Human Rights Act and replace it with a British Bill of Rights so decisions are taken in British courts.	Supports the Human Rights Act.
A fair deal for England	Will stop MPs from Scotland, Wales & Northern Ireland voting on English laws.	Is happy for MPs from Scotland, Wales and Northern Ireland to vote on English laws.

Not sure who to vote for?

MAY 7

A leaflet we delivered to every home in the constituency on the morning of Saturday 18 April, contrasting my views with those of Sarah Jones, and David Cameron's with Ed Miliband's.

The alternative #BackBarwell2015 poster that we encouraged shopkeepers to display in their windows.

Acknowledgements

NUMEROUS FAMILY MEMBERS, friends and colleagues in the whips' office kindly took the time to read the first draft of this book and offer their thoughts. In particular, my friend Peter Goddard's comments were crucial in turning what was initially three or four different stories into one book and lightening and tightening the text. I'm also grateful to Olivia Beattie and Jonathan Wadman at Biteback for their comments on the second draft. Their eagle eyes spotted a number of inconsistencies as well as passages where further explanation was required. Having not written a book before, I didn't always find feedback on something so close to my heart easy to receive, but in hindsight the book is much the better for it. Any remaining errors are of course my own.

Finally, my thanks to Iain Dale and Biteback for agreeing to publish something that was originally intended as a story for my children to read when they're a bit older, and to Sunil and Balraj Tandon, Badsha Quadir, Derek Galloway, Colin and Delia Hart,

Raj Rajeswaran, Matthew Taylor, Ravi Shankar and Simon Brew for their generosity in making it possible.

GAVIN BARWELL

CROYDON

JANUARY 2016